J

Concepts
in
Problem Solving

Moshe F. Rubinstein
Kenneth R. Pfeiffer

Concepts
in
Problem Solving

Prentice-Hall, Inc., Englewood Cliffs, NJ 07632

Library of Congress Cataloging in Publication Data

Rubinstein, Moshe F
   Concepts in problem solving.

   Bibliography: p.
   Includes Index.
   1. Problem solving. 2. Uncertainty. 3. Decision-making.
I. Pfeiffer, Kenneth R., joint author. II. Title.
H91.R8   300'.1'8   79-4391
ISBN 0-13-166603-7

Interior design and editorial/production supervision by Steven Bobker
Cover design by Jerry Pfeiffer
Manufacturing buyer: Gordon Osbourne

10 9 8 7 6 5 4 3 2 1

Printed in the United States of America

Prentice-Hall International, Inc., *London*
Prentice-Hall of Australia Pty. Limited, *Sydney*
Prentice-Hall of Canada, Ltd., *Toronto*
Prentice-Hall of India Private Limited, *New Delhi*
Prentice-Hall of Japan, Inc., *Tokyo*
Prentice-Hall of Southeast Asia Pte. Ltd., *Singapore*
Whitehall Books Limited, *Wellington, New Zealand*

לאחי דוד רובינשטיין

Contents

contents

4

Introduction to decision making *133*

5

Dealing with Conflict Situations *165*

edge presented in the book to different areas. We have avoided abstract theoretical discussions, so as not to obscure the relevance of the material. The text is written as a story to enhance readibility and emphasize applications. There is a dialogue throughout the text between Professor Gordian and his nephew Alex in which we have anticipated and answered many questions that might occur to readers while studying the material.

The book can be useful as an introduction to other courses. For example, it can serve as an introduction to a probability and statistics class or to a class in decision theory or game theory. The terminology and practical application of concepts that are introduced will aid the reader in grasping and applying more advanced material.

The following is a brief survey of the book's contents. Chapter 1 presents models of the problem solving process and emphasizes the role of human values. Common failings in problem solving are identified. General precepts and guides to aid the problem solver are discussed.

Chapter 2 proceeds from a discussion of natural language and its ambiguities to symbolic logic and its special features. Important tools of problem representation are introduced and the role of models in problem solving in general is discussed.

Chapter 3 treats information, its quantitative measurement, and the assessment of its relevance in dispelling uncertainty. The basic premise is that a *Will to Doubt* is essential for proper assimilation of information. Concepts from probability theory are developed. These concepts are used to quantify uncertainty in problem situations such as gambling, business, and the results of diagnostic tests.

Chapter 4 introduces decision making models, including: elements of decision theory; utility theory and the measurement of values; types of decision makers; decisions with partial information; and decisions with conflicting objectives.

Chapter 5 provides the framework for creating models for decision making in conflict situations. It includes: elements of game theory; the role of human values in making decisions under conflict; and applications to business, personal conflicts, crime and punishment in society, and distribution of wealth.

The chapters generally stand as independent units and may be read in any order, except that some knowledge of probability as presented in Chapter 3, Part 1, is helpful before studying material in Chapters 4 and 5.

We have included a number of study aids in the book. The

Preface

Our experience of more than a decade with a campuswide problem solving course at UCLA has allowed us to identify a core of key concepts that may serve as a framework in designing a problem solving course. We have come to realize that it is not practical to rigidly specify course content for a variety of different students, instructors, and institutions. Therefore, the framework we have identified gives instructors a foundation upon which to build a course that incorporates experiences, philosophies, and attitudes that are most appropriate for the students in a particular institution. This makes it possible to include personal creative efforts in the design of a course in problem solving.

Concepts in Problem Solving is supplemented by a manual for instructors that includes a teaching guide and solutions to the problems in the text.

The purpose of this book is to present fundamental topics in problem solving in a way that is easy to digest and that can be readily generalized to diverse real-world situations. The emphasis is on applications of basic and important tools to actual problems a person might encounter in everyday life. These applications make the material more usable, and help the reader transfer the knowl-

Storylike Presentation sparks interest and aids in the retention and application of knowledge to relevant situations. *Marginal Notations* emphasize key concepts and ideas throughout the text. These notations serve as an aid for review, and make the text more useful as a reference source. Liberal use of *Figures and Illustrations* is made throughout the text. *Problems and Suggested Projects* are provided with each chapter and are keyed to the particular section to which they refer. *Answers and Partial Solutions* to selected problems appear at the end of the book to provide feedback in the learning process.

The material in this book can serve as an introduction to more advanced topics in problem solving that appear in *Patterns of Problem Solving* by Moshe F. Rubinstein, Prentice Hall, 1975.

Moshe F. Rubinstein

Kenneth R. Pfeiffer

acknowledgments

We are indebted to Kim E. Burroughs for her original artwork appearing in Chapter 1. We also appreciate her helpful suggestions and editorial assistance throughout seemingly endless readings of the manuscript. Her devotion, patience, and support greatly contributed to the authors' mood and the quality of the work.

Zaffa, Iris, and Dorit served as the testing grounds for many ideas, stories, and anecdotes that are incorporated in the book. Their similar experience with earlier books was invaluable in developing *Concepts in Problem Solving*.

Gary Gasca was helpful in contributing to discussions of various topics in the early stages of developing the ideas for the book.

We benefitted greatly from the response to preliminary versions of the material by participants in the NSF Chautauqua-Type Short Course on Patterns of Problem Solving, and participants in special seminars on Problem Solving. The warm and encouraging response of these outstanding people from academia and industry provided the incentive for writing the book.

1

Guides to Problem Solving

Alex jumped out of his car and walked happily up the stairs to his uncle's house. He was excited because he and his uncle were going to the mountains for the weekend so that his uncle could teach him how to cross-country ski. His uncle, Professor Robert Gordian, was a well-liked instructor at the nearby university. Professor Gordian greeted Alex at the door with a big smile and the usual playful twinkle in his eyes. It was clear to Alex that his uncle was no less pleased than himself.

"All set?" Professor Gordian asked.

"Yep!" Alex replied. "Put your stuff in the car and we're off!"

They had decided to take Alex's car, an aging van, because Professor Gordian's car, a VW bug, was not large enough for their suitcases, skis, and assorted paraphernalia. After loading their things into the van, they jumped in and putted off. They had planned to drive to the professor's cabin that afternoon, and spend the next two days skiing before returning home Sunday evening.

Alex and his uncle got along wonderfully. They were both avid fishermen and in the summer they often went to a lake in the same mountains to go fishing. To refresh the conversation after it had lagged for awhile, Alex said, "I remember you saying that you were teaching a new course this term, but I forgot what it was about. Wasn't it about problems or something?"

"It's a course in problem solving," his uncle replied. "It's a new type of course in which students are exposed to a variety of tools that might generally be helpful in solving problems. It's very different because it doesn't focus on a specific subject discipline, but instead attempts to apply to all types of problems. These problems might range from math or puzzles, to a choice of a career, or to broad-reaching social problems, like pollution.

"I see," said Alex, "but I don't really understand what a math problem has in common with a problem like choosing a career."

"Well," replied Professor Gordian, "all problems have in common the condition that 'what is' is not the same as 'what is desired.' I think I can make this a little clearer for you by showing you a model."

Professor Gordian pulled a piece of paper and a pencil from his pocket. Alex, expecting him to start folding a paper airplane, said with a puzzled look on his face, "What? Now I'm really confused. What do paper planes have to do with problems?"

model Professor Gordian smiled and replied, "By model I mean something much more general than what you are used to. A model is an abstract representation of reality. If I fold a paper plane, that would be a type of model because it represents a real airplane. It is abstract in the sense that only some of the qualities of a real airplane are represented, like its ability to fly. But there are other types of models as well. For example, a roadmap is a model. It is abstract because things like street lights and stop signs are not represented, and because it uses lines instead of concrete and asphalt. It is a representation of reality because the relationships among the lines represent the relationships among streets. You can tell how to get from one place to another by seeing what lines lead to where."

Professor Gordian drew the diagram in Figure 1 on the sheet of paper and handed it to Alex. As Alex glanced at the diagram, Pro-

model of a problem in general

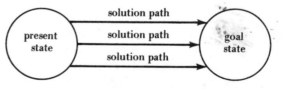

Figure 1. Model of a problem in general.

fessor Gordian explained, "The circle on the left represents the present state; that is, 'what is.' The circle on the right represents the goal state, or 'what is desired.' There are usually several different ways to reach the goal state from the present state, and these are called solution paths. Although this model has a specific form, you can fit into it many different contents in the way of different types of problems. I'll show you. Give me a problem."

Alex thought for a minute, and replied, "OK, $X^2 + 5X + 8 = 2$. Find X."

Professor Gordian responded, "The equation you've just presented is the present state. The goal state is to have some expression where X = a specific number or numbers. There are several possible solution paths. You could subtract 2 from both sides of the equation and factor, or you could use the general quadratic formula

$$X = \frac{-B \pm \sqrt{B^2 - 4AC}}{2A}$$

"Now give me another problem."

Alex thought for another moment, and said, "What about what I'm going to do for a career?"

"Here the present state is your uncertainty about what you are going to do with your life. The goal state is for you to have a satisfying career, and the solution paths are for you to pursue any of a number of satisfying careers. In this problem, you want to pick the best available solution path."

"Hey! That's a pretty neat way of looking at things!" exclaimed Alex. "I can see how using a model would make problem solving easier because it forces you to make clear what you have and what you want, as well as all the different alternatives. Something puzzles me though. A minute ago you said the model you drew had a specific form into which a lot of different contents could be fit. What did you mean by the words 'form' and 'content'?"

"The form of a model," replied Professor Gordian," is its *method* of representation, which may be verbal, pictorial, mathematical, a material object, or even a combination of one or more of these if that's what you want. It's up to the person doing the modeling to pick which method or methods would work the best for his particular problem. Since all models are representations, then all models must have a *method* of representation, or a form.

"form" of a model

3

"content"
of a model
"The other fundamental feature of all models is that they have a content, in other words, *something which is to be represented.* The content can be anything or everything depending on what you want your model to do."

"Now I understand," replied Alex. "Are there any other kinds of models that apply to all problems?"

model of
problem
solving
process
Professor Gordian replied, "Yes, there is a fairly well accepted model for what people do in trying to solve problems. This model has a different form from the one we have just talked about. It is a verbal model which is just a description of a thing or process in words. The model says that when presented with a problem, people first perceive and analyze the problem components. Next, they formulate various hypotheses, or possible solutions. Then they look at these hypotheses and throw out the least plausible ones. Finally, they subject the most likely hypotheses to very close scrutiny to try to decide which is best. This could yield a satisfactory solution, but sometimes no solution can be reached immediately. In the event no solution is quickly found, people incubate. You can think of this as sitting on your ideas until they hatch. After you have thought about a problem extensively and have not come to a satisfying solution, you might forget about it and go about doing something else. Very often, the solution will come to you in a flash of insight while you are doing something entirely unrelated to the problem. Remember the story I told you about Archimedes running naked through the streets shouting 'Eureka! I've found it!'? He had been taking a bath when he discovered the solution to a famous problem in physics that he had been thinking about for a long time.

"Of course, errors are possible at any of the stages of problem solving. A person might not see the problem components in a useful fashion, he might not think of any fruitful hypotheses, or he might make an error when evaluating the hypotheses. You might try a problem and see if this model gives an accurate description of what goes on in your head."

"Yes," replied Alex, "that seems to be what I do when I try to solve a problem. I look at the problem, think of various things to try, and then pick the best solution. I can see how useful models are. They really help a person's understanding of something."

Professor Gordian nodded and said, "Yes, Alex, they do. Models are also useful as aids to prediction. For example, physics is a model of reality. And you can use physics to predict what will happen if you do various things in the real world. With understanding and prediction comes the possibility of control. Models are fundamental to our understanding and dealing with reality: The more we understand, the better we can predict, and the better we can predict, the greater the possibility of control."

Alex listened attentively, and when Professor Gordian was through he asked, "One thing particularly interests me in that model of how people solve problems—incubation. How does that work?"

"No one knows for sure how incubation works, but there are many possible explanations. One explanation holds that after you've been working on a problem for a long time, you might be very close to a solution but have become too tired to actually reach the correct answer. Incubation could provide a rest period in which the fatigue would dissipate, and allow you to come to the solution. Another explanation could be that the problem solver might be fixated on an inappropriate solution path. Incubation could allow him to step back and look at the problem from a fresh viewpoint. Another type of explanation brings into play the role of the subconscious mind. Some people think that in consciously attempting to solve a problem, most people use the left side of their brain. The left brain works in a logical, sequential, analytic fashion. But the solution to many types of problems requires a kind of total picture approach called holistic. — incubation

"It is felt the right brain operates in just such a fashion. When you stop thinking about a problem consciously, the right brain might start to work on it in an entirely different way. Incubation might work by allowing the subconscious mind to play a role via 'right brain' thought."

"That's fascinating," said Alex. "I'm getting very interested in your course. It sounds like it might be very scientific. Do you teach any sure-fire approaches to solving all problems?"

"No, Alex. Problem solving is much too subjective for that. The mere fact that incubation exists suggests that intuition and perhaps chance play important roles in solving some problems. In addition, there are classes of emotional, cultural, and environmental factors that hinder a person's ability to solve many problems. You may — environmental constraint
have difficulty solving a problem because there are distractions around you. Or you might not be able to solve a problem because — emotional constraint
you're afraid of people laughing at your proposed solution. You might be much more comfortable judging proposed solutions than

5

generating your own. You might not even be able to think of any solution under adverse circumstances. To illustrate another of these factors, take this problem. You are in a room with six other people. The problem is to remove a ping pong ball from a pipe imbedded in a concrete floor. The ball is resting on the floor inside the pipe. The pipe extends four inches above the floor, and has an inside diameter a tiny bit larger than the ball. You have the following tools: a hammer, a file, a wire coat hanger, and a monkey wrench. You must remove the ball without damaging the ball, the pipe, or the floor. Take a few minutes and try to think of as many ways as you can to get the ball out."

Alex remained silent for several minutes, and then said, "Well, so far I can only think of two ways of getting the ball out. I could take the coat hanger and unbend it to form a big pair of tweezers. After I filed down the ends, I could probably reach inside the pipe and grasp the ball and remove it."

"Very clever!" complimented Alex's uncle, "and what was your other method of solution?"

"I could take the monkey wrench and smash the handle of the hammer and perhaps use the splinters as tweezers."

cultural constraint "That is another inventive idea! I'm sure you'll be surprised when I tell you that there is a way of removing the ball without using any of the tools. I'm also sure that you will see that you didn't think of it because of a cultural taboo that exists in our society."

Alex knitted his brow in deep thought. Again he was silent for several minutes. He drove into a gas station and as he pulled up in front of the gas pump, he laughed out loud. "Oh no! You mean they could pee in the pipe and float the ball out?"

"Ha!" laughed the professor, "You guessed it! Most people don't think of this because urinating is a private activity, not to be mentioned or thought about in public."

Alex jumped out of his car and while the attendant was pumping gas, he fiddled considerably with his van, adding water, oil, and making adjustments under the hood. All the while, he was thinking about what his uncle had said: that many personal and subjective factors enter into the solution of problems. He thought that if one could become aware of all of the interfering tendencies in problem solving one might be able somehow to counteract them.

After paying the attendant, Alex got back into his car and they started down the highway again. When they were well under way, Alex asked his uncle, "So would you say that instead of teaching specific methods of solving problems, you attempt to develop in students a critical and perceptive attitude?"

"Well, yes and no, Alex. The proper attitude toward problem solving is very important. As an example, I try to get students away from the 'let's just get it over with' attitude that is so prevalent, by replacing it with an attitude of wanting to create a *good* solution. A good solution is one that frequently requires time and effort when compared to a solution that gets a problem off your back but that might later create more problems than it solves. But there are also many specific methods and tools that I try to get across to students. For example, there are models which might be important no matter what the type of problem, and there are some specific attitudes that are useful in solving nearly any type of problem. For instance, one attitude is to have the will to doubt. Many people, when approaching a problem, will come up with an alternative that they think is the best solution. When evaluating other alternatives, the evidence that is examined will tend to be biased against these other alternatives and toward their favored alternative. This leads to a distortion of reality and the best solution is not reached. One should approach each problem with as open a mind as possible, and admit that even though an alternative looks good now, that might change with the introduction of new evidence. This is the same thing as being able to admit that you're wrong. This attitude, in my mind, is extremely valuable to develop, not only in problem solving but in one's evaluation of all things, personal and social. Keeping a will to doubt fights dogmatism and prejudice and enhances the ability to correct your own mistakes by stressing the importance of continued learning and improvement. An example of what I'm talking about is stereotyping. Stereotypes are useful in the sense that a correct stereotype tells you something about a specific instance in the absence of other information. But a stereotype only tells you what something *probably* is like. All things are different, and there are exceptions to every rule. Stereotypes often blind a person to the individuality of a specific instance, and prevent one from properly evaluating evidence about some particular case. This can be combatted by having a will to doubt, or by withholding judgment until there is enough evidence to be able to arrive at a well considered conclusion."

have a will to doubt

stereotyping

withhold judgment

While Alex was mulling that over, the professor brought out a sack lunch that he had packed for them and they both started munching sandwiches and fruit. As they started up a slight grade, a loud knocking sound emerged from the engine.

"Darn this car!" exclaimed Alex, "Now the ignition timing is off! Something new happens every week. We'll be lucky if we make it for another ten miles."

"What makes you think that the ignition timing is off?" asked the professor.

"Well, isn't engine knock an indication that your timing is too far advanced?"

whole
picture

"Sometimes that's true, but many factors combine to determine what the correct setting for the timing is. Perhaps you're rushing your judgment and thereby not seeing the whole picture. A common failing in problem solving is a difficulty in isolating the problem. Can you think of any other reasons for your engine knocking?"

"Hmmm. You're right. We did just fill up with a cheap brand of gas. Perhaps it could be a low octane fuel that's causing the ping. I can't really say whether it's the gas, or that the timing has changed. I do know though that I have a problem with my car. It's a wreck as you can plainly see. It burns oil, the radiator leaks, it gets poor gas mileage, the shocks are worn out, the tires are practically gone, and there are a hundred other problems. I've thought about getting a new car, but I just read in *Consumer Reports* that the most economical thing to do is to fix an old car and run it into the ground. I don't know which to do."

talk about
problem

"You definitely have a problem, Alex. Perhaps I can help. One of the best things you can do when you have a problem is to talk about it. Different people have different experiences and perspectives on things, and someone else can often add something that you wouldn't readily see yourself. It also helps just to explain your problem to someone else, because in order to explain something you have to have a pretty good understanding of it, and you have to be able to express it in words. Several times I've thought that I understood a concept, but when it came to telling it to someone else, I quickly learned that I didn't understand it at all! This can be extremely embarrassing when you are standing in front of a large class! There is an old saying, 'In order to truly understand something you have to teach it to someone else first.'

"Suppose we start on your problem. What might you do first in attempting to solve it?"

Alex thought for a minute, mulling over his uncle's words. "I could make a model of my problem!"

"Good idea!" What sort of model do you have in mind?"

"How about using the general model of a problem that you told me about?"

"That sounds like a good idea. What is your present state?"

"My car is a wreck."

"OK, and what is the goal state?"

"Having a better car!"

"That sounds pretty good, but be careful, Alex. The initial representation of a problem is the most important step. It is crucial that a lot of time and care be spent at this stage, because otherwise you might develop more problems than you solve. Do you remember the old Rube Goldberg contraptions? I remember one where you could pull out your tooth by tickling a bird, whose convulsions of laughter mixed the contents of a cocktail shaker, and then when the bird fell forward the cocktail was spilled onto a squirrel in a running cage who got drunk and ran, turning a phonograph, and so on and so on until a cannon was fired which extracted the tooth by a string attached to the cannonball. Clearly there are better ways to extract teeth. You need to make sure that you are asking the appropriate question." Professor Gordian slipped down in his seat a bit and chuckled. "This reminds me of a friend of mine who is a clergyman. He's a smoker, but was concerned about the religious propriety of smoking when he prayed. When he asked his superior whether or not it was all right to smoke while praying, he got a resounding no. But I often wonder what the

initial representation

ask appropriate questions

Figure 2. Rube Goldberg contraption.

answer would have been had he asked if it was all right to pray while he smoked. Very often the question asked determines the answer received. In your case, suppose you had phrased your problem as what kind of new car to get. You would then have restricted yourself and you wouldn't have even considered fixing your old car. You might not have achieved the best solution for yourself. Can you think of another formulation for your goal state, one that is not so restrictive?"

Alex nodded thoughtfully and replied, "How about having a reliable mode of transportation?"

"That sounds better. Now how about some possible solution paths?"

"OK. I've already mentioned two—fixing my old car and buying a new one. Let's see . . . I could buy a used car. Or, I could get a motorcycle! I see what you mean now about the initial formulation of the problem determining the range of choices!"

explore all plausible alternatives "Good! Perhaps I can make a suggestion. In the initial stages at least, it is often helpful to explore all plausible alternatives. Try to abandon any preconceived notions that you might have and think up all reasonable solution paths. Now, can you think of any more?"

"Well, let's see. I could ride a bike, or I could even walk! I could hitchhike, I could get rides with friends, I could use a skateboard, or I could use roller skates."

consider values at all stages "Now you're getting the idea. The point is to not limit yourself at the beginning. You might find it instructive here to notice the role of values in problem solving. Different people can use the same tools to solve the same problem and come up with entirely different solutions because their values are different. Values enter into the problem solving process at all three stages of the model; present state, goal state, and solution paths. Your evaluation of the present state, that your car is a wreck, is an evaluation due to your particular values. Your kid brother thinks your car is swell! Your evaluation of what constitutes a reliable and safe mode of transportation is likewise a function of your own values. For some people, a reliable form of transportation would be nothing less than a $50,000 Rolls Royce! For others, merely their good health and sound feet would suffice. Some may consider a skateboard unsafe at any speed. Clearly your values enter into your selection of the best solution path, and even your list of possible ones. This incorporation of human values in the problem solving process is another reason why it is difficult to formulate any sure-fire procedures for solving all problems. The problem solving process must be individualized for any given person because personal values are unique."

"That's something that I hadn't thought about before, but it certainly makes sense. So by taking into account my own values, I can now go on to select the best solution path for me. Let me figure out what the logical next step should be. I already have a model and have formulated several different solution paths. Hey, this is just like the model for the general problem solving process! I think the next step should be to throw out some of the more unreasonable solution paths and to select the best ones for more detailed consideration."

"That sounds logical," Professor Gordian agreed.

"Right away I think I could rule out all of the alternatives like walking or riding a bike, because I usually have so many things to carry. I have to carry books and papers to school. I have to carry groceries home from the market, and my job delivering pizzas would be difficult and unsafe on a skateboard. My job also rules out a motorcycle or depending on getting rides from others. That leaves only getting a new car, getting a used car, or fixing my old car. What I need to do now is to determine which alternative will be the cheapest."

Professor Gordian raised his eyebrows. "Is that all you are concerned with? Have you gotten the whole picture? Suppose that you found that the cheapest thing to do was to get a particular used car that was a smog belching, loud, flame-emblazoned chariot with no doors or bumpers?" *whole picture*

Alex smiled sheepishly. "Yes, I get the picture. There are more things in life than money. I will need to consider a large number of things."

"Quite right. In your analysis, it might help to also consider the problem from the viewpoint of others, like your parents, your friends, your girl friend, your boss, and the police, just to name a few, along with the values of society as a whole." *viewpoint of others*

"I can see that I have quite a job ahead of me. Can you offer any suggestions that might make it easier?"

"For most problems, it is of immense benefit to write things down. You already have a model, you could write that down. You are going to have to consider many different factors in your decision, so you should write them down too. Writing things down helps in a number of ways. First of all, you can only remember a limited number of things in a short period of time. The limit of short term memory is seven plus or minus two unrelated items. If *write things down* *limit of memory* the amount of information exceeds that, then you will not be able to use all of it simultaneously.

"One of the most common failings in problem solving is the failure to utilize known information. Sometimes this results from a memory overload. You can circumvent this by using artificial memory devices, the most convenient of which is pencil and paper. Writing things down also helps you to focus on the important elements in your problem and helps you remember intermediate inferences and subgoals along the way to the final solution."

"That sounds like a good idea! I had better wait until later to finish this problem, though, because it looks like right now I'm going to have to devote all my attention to driving."

As they had been ascending into the mountains, the road had become icy in patches. The bald tires of the old van were slipping and sliding and it took all of Alex's attention to keep the car on the road. Several times the van fishtailed, but Alex was able to recover. Later, while going around a curve, Alex was not so fortunate and the van slid out and spun around 270°, ending up with the rear wheels stuck in a ditch. They both breathed a sigh of relief that the van had not overturned. But their relief was short lived as Alex discovered that he could not extricate the van from the ditch. He tried going forward, going backward, and rocking back and forth, all to no avail.

"Well, Uncle, it looks like we have a real problem now. How are we going to get out of this ditch?"

"Good question, Alex, but don't despair. There are usually many more resources available than are immediately apparent."

Alex hoped that his uncle was right, as the road they were on was very seldom traveled and it might be a long time before anyone would happen by to help pull them out. Professor Gordian stepped out of the van and surveyed the situation. Then he looked into the back of the van, standing there with a faraway look in his eyes and muttering to himself. He picked up Alex's large bumper jack and looked it over carefully. Then he picked up a coil of rope, tied it to a tree on the other side of the road, and brought the loose end back to the van. He brought the jack to the front of the van and removed the handle and head from the standard. Then he cut a smaller piece of rope and tied the base of the jack to the front bumper. He tied the head of the jack to the piece of rope that was around the tree. Then he put the head of the jack back on the standard, but upside down. Everything is shown in Figure 3. Suddenly it dawned on Alex what the Professor was up to.

Figure 3. The van in the ditch!

"You're going to jack the head of the jack *down* the standard and the whole thing is going to act like a winch and pull us out of the ditch!"

"Right you are Alex, *if* all goes according to plan."

As the professor jacked, the car rose out of the ditch. Alex couldn't hide his amazement.

"Uncle, how did you ever think of using the jack like that?"

"Most things can have many different functions even though people usually use them for only one thing. The inability to see things as having more than the usual function is a common deter- **functional** rent in problem solving called functional fixation. This was first **fixation** investigated by Karl Duncker, a psychologist interested in problem solving. He discovered that functional fixation was a result of people's experience with objects. For example, in one experiment, he put subjects in a room with two strings hanging from the ceiling. Their task was to tie the two ends of the string together. But when a subject took hold of one of the strings and walked over to get the other string, the distance between them was sufficiently great so that he couldn't reach it." Professor Gordian illustrated the situation by drawing in the snow with a stick (See Figure 4). "The subjects also had some tools to help them. They had a pair of pliers, some paperclips, and some sheets of typing paper. What do you think you would do in a situation like this, Alex?"

13

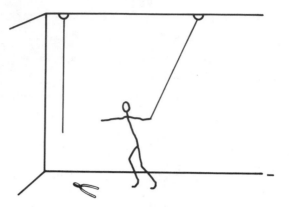

Figure 4. Tie the strings together.

Alex thought over the situation for a moment and then exclaimed "Oh, I see! You could tie the pliers to the end of one string and start it swinging like a pendulum. Then when you grab the other string and walk over, the pendulum will come to you and you could tie the strings together."

"Very good, Alex. Many subjects in this experiment didn't see that the problem could be solved in this manner. Interestingly, Duncker found that if the subjects had just been involved in a task where they had to fix a piece of electrical apparatus using the pliers to bend wire, they were even worse at solving this problem than those subjects that had no such experience. Thus, Duncker inferred that experience with an object in a limited variety of situations prevents you from seeing other uses for that object."

"But you were aware of that tendency and were able to overcome it?"

"Well, not exactly. I wish I could take credit for that invention, but I seem to remember having seen it in a magazine somewhere."

Still impressed, Alex helped his uncle load the rope and jack back into the van before they were on their way again. It soon became necessary for them to stop again and put on tire chains because the road had been transformed into a solid sheet of glare ice. Everything passed uneventfully until they came to the long driveway up to the cabin. The driveway was quite steep and was covered with very hard and smooth ice. As they tried to drive up, the van began to slip, even with the tire chains. Several times they took a run at the driveway, but each time, about one quarter of the way up, they would lose traction and the tires would spin helplessly.

Alex turned to the professor with a look of surrender on his face. "Oh well, it looks like we get to take a long hike with all of our gear."

"Not necessarily, Alex. Although it looks as though we can't drive up the driveway, that isn't the only way to get to the house."

Alex looked over toward the cabin. The ground was covered with only a thin layer of well consolidated snow. He suddenly realized what the professor was talking about.

"It's peculiar that would never have occurred to me if I were by myself," he said, as he drove off the road and across the snow to the cabin.

"That is an example of another common hindrance in problem solving. This one is called an associational constraint. You couldn't solve the problem because you were limiting the problem area too closely. You were making unnecessary assumptions that hindered your problem solving by causing you to not consider a viable alternative. Here is another illustration of the same tendency." Professor Gordian pulled out a piece of paper and his pencil, and drew nine dots in a square pattern, as in Figure 5a. "OK, Alex, can you draw four straight lines that go through all nine dots without lifting the pencil from the paper?" **associational constraint**

Alex took the paper and pencil, and several times tried to draw lines through the dots. After each attempt, he gave up with a shrug. Then he muttered something to himself about limiting himself too much. Suddenly he smiled and drew the correct solution on the paper. With a look of pride he grinned at Professor Gordian and said, "It's very hard not to make unnecessary assumptions in some situations!"

After they had unpacked and settled comfortably in the cabin, Professor Gordian started preparing dinner while Alex built a fire. Alex had found some kindling in the cabin and had the rudiments

Figure 5a. The nine dot problem.

15

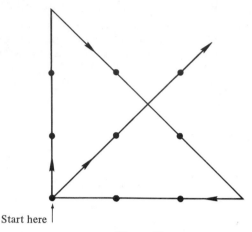

Start here

Figure 5b.

of a satisfactory blaze going when he went outside to get some more substantial logs. There he discovered the woodpile submerged in snow. When he tried to pull out some logs he found them frozen securely in place. He tried pounding and prying with his axe but to no avail. Going back into the cabin, he enlisted his uncle's help.

When Professor Gordian went outside and surveyed the situation, he said to Alex, "This is an interesting problem, mainly because it reminds me of another problem we had recently. One thing that you might do when confronted with a new problem is to see if it is like any other problem that you have already solved. That can at least give you some ideas on how you might begin. In the same vein, you might try to use analogies or metaphors to suggest some new ideas. Does this problem remind you of one that you have already solved?"

Alex looked puzzled and scratched the back of his neck. Hesitatingly, he said, "It does sort of remind me of when we got stuck in the ditch today. You know, the proverbial immovable object. What if I rigged up the jack to that tree over there and pulled these logs apart?"

Professor Gordian looked approvingly at Alex. "It sounds like it should work. Let me know what happens. It's cold out here!" He rushed back inside.

Alex was indeed successful with the jack. After they had eaten and cleared the table, they pulled the round table over in front of

similar problems

analogies and metaphors

the fire and played a few hands of poker. Then Professor Gordian proposed a change. "Alex, what if we play a new game. Let's alternate placing poker chips on this flat saucer. You can place a chip anywhere on the saucer you like, as long as it does not overlap any other chip or hang off the edge. The last person who can place a chip on the saucer wins."

"OK, Uncle, it sounds like fun. But knowing you there's probably some trick involved. Before I lose a lot of money, why don't you level with me? What's the trick?"

Professor Gordian laughed. "Yes, I guess there is a trick. Let me tell you this. If each player uses the best plays available to him, one player will always win, and it is either the player who plays first or the player who plays second. Can you figure out which it is?"

Alex thought for a minute and then walked over to the desk in the living room.

"Where are you going, Alex?" asked Professor Gordian.

"I'm going to get a ruler so I can figure this out," answered Alex, matter of factly.

"But you don't need a ruler. You can figure it out just by thinking about it."

"But the answer has got to depend on the relative sizes of the saucer and poker chips!" asserted Alex, dismayed.

"Not so. Regardless of the size of the chips and saucer, the same player always wins."

Alex walked back to the table, incredulous. He plumped himself down in his chair and stared blankly at the table, his mouth open. "I just don't get it," he said.

"This is a problem that can be solved by looking at a special case, and then generalizing to all cases. Suppose that the saucer was small compared to the poker chip, so that only one chip could be placed on the saucer. Who would win?" *specializing and generalizing*

"Obviously the first player. But the saucer is much larger than that! How does your case apply?"

"Well, take another case. Suppose the saucer could accommodate two chips, side by side. Who would win then?"

"Then the sec. . ." Alex blurted and then stopped. "No! the first player would still win if he put his chip in the middle of the saucer."

"Correct! Now suppose you were the first player and always placed your first chip in the middle, regardless of the size of the saucer. Your opponent would have to place his chip somewhere.

17

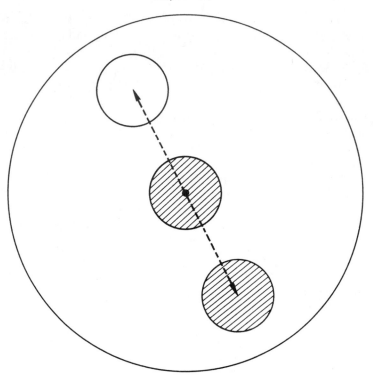

Figure 6. The poker chip game.

Now notice (see Figure 6). If there is room for your opponent to place a chip, there will always be room for a chip diametrically opposite where he places his chip."

"So the first player plays his chip to the center and then plays opposite to where the second player plays, and the first player will always win! Amazing!" Alex stared into the fire in wonder.

"Of course, there are more mundane examples of how this same problem solving strategy will work. Try this one. One thousand twenty five tennis players participate in a single elimination tournament. How many single games of tennis need to be played before there emerge one winner and one thousand twenty four losers?"

"You mean that when a game is played, the loser is eliminated and the winner goes on to play again until he loses once or wins the whole tournament?"

"Exactly," replied the professor.

"This looks like one of those problems that you just have to grind through. Since there are 1025 players, in the first round one player sits out and the remaining players pair off and play 512 games. Then the winners of those games play 256 games and so on. This is one of those problems where writing it down is certain to be helpful!"

"That's true, if you choose to work it in the way you have suggested. But try looking at a special case, say with just a few players, and then see if you can generalize."

"All right. Suppose there were only two players. It would clearly take only one game. If there were three players, one would sit out while the other two played, and then the winner would play the person who sat out. That makes two games. If there were four players, they would pair off and the winners of the first two games would meet to decide the overall champion. That is three games. With five players, it's the same as with four players but one player sits out, so there would be four games. So it looks like there is one fewer game played than the number of players. With 1025 players there should be 1024 games!"

"See how useful that strategy is? If you recall, that is the same strategy that is used in mathematical induction. You prove a statement true for $N = 1$, a special case, and then you allow generalization to all cases by showing that if it is true for N then it is true for $N + 1$."

"Yes, I recall learning about math induction in school. Tell me, do you know of any other useful tricks like that?"

"There are quite a few common strategies that can be tried when one gets stuck on a problem. Take this problem, for instance." Professor Gordian went to the closet and brought out a checkerboard and a box of dominoes. "Notice that I can take the checkerboard and cover all sixty four squares with thirty two dominoes. Now suppose I remove two squares at opposite corners of the checkerboard." Professor Gordian tore off two small squares from his napkin and placed them on the upper right and lower left corners of the checkerboard. "Can I cover the remaining 62 squares with thirty one dominoes?"

"Hmmm. My first impression would be to say 'yes'. But, I'm not sure. How would you go about showing whether you could or couldn't?"

"To show that it can be done, all you would have to do is to do it! It would seem more difficult to show that it cannot be done. But in fact there is a strategy called the *method of contradiction* that can be particularly useful in cases like this. The method of contradiction is familiar to most people who have taken elemen-

method of
contradiction

tary geometry. You start out by making an assumption. You then follow this assumption through to its logical conclusion. By the rules of logic, if the original assumption is true, then any logical consequence of it must be true. If it turns out, however, that you find some false statement or contradiction, then something must be wrong. It cannot be the rules of logic, so it must be that your initial assumption is false.

"This is a very powerful tool but it bothers many people who are unfamiliar with it. Not only do you have to start by assuming the opposite of what you want to show, but the first time many people see this method is in high school geometry. They think that if the method is so useful, then why haven't they seen it before then? Actually, people use it subconsciously quite often. For example, suppose that you are indoors and you want to determine whether or not it is raining. From your window you can see only the ground, not the sky. If you assume it is raining, then it follows that the ground must be wet. You check the ground and it isn't wet. This is a contradiction. Therefore, your initial assumption that it's raining must be false. You could also take a problem in elementary geometry. Given the assumption that two distinct points determine one and only one straight line, prove that two lines can intersect at no more than one point. First assume the opposite of what you want to show. Assume that two lines can intersect at more than one point, say two points. Then from the initial assumption, these two points determine one and only one straight line. But here you have a contradiction. Therefore, your initial assumption must be false, and it follows that the lines can intersect at no more than one point."

"I remember having seen this method before. Let's see how it applies to the problem at hand. Since I am going to try to show that it is not possible to cover the board with 31 dominoes, I'll start out by assuming that it is possible. Now I want to arrive at some kind of contradiction. Hmm. . ."

Alex pondered over the problem and the professor sat back and watched quietly.

Alex continued, "A domino covers one black and one white square. So thirty one dominoes cover 31 black and 31 white squares. Aha! A normal checkerboard has 32 black and 32 white squares and when you changed the checkerboard, you removed two *black* squares! There are 30 black squares and 32 white squares left. There is my contradiction! It can't be done."

"Excellent, excellent!" beamed Professor Gordian.

By this time they were very tired after the long and tedious drive, so they went to bed and slept soundly until the morning.

*   *   *   *

While having breakfast the next morning Professor Gordian explained the fine points of ski touring and Alex listened attentively. Since Alex was in fine physical condition and was also an excellent downhill skier, neither of them thought that there would be any difficulty in his learning Nordic ski touring. It was a beautiful day when they left the cabin. It was sunny, clear and about 20°F (−7°C). The snow was cold, dry, and compacted—perfect conditions. As they skied on the flat ground through the trees Alex had no difficulty keeping up. Professor Gordian frequently glanced rearward to see how Alex was doing. As they came to the edge of the trees, there was a long clear downhill run. Professor Gordian turned to Alex and reminded him of the limitations of the Nordic ski touring equipment, noting that most of the advanced downhill techniques used with Alpine skis were usually just not possible with Nordic skis. He demonstrated the snowplow turn and the stem turn, and Alex repeated them easily at the top of the hill. With this preparation, Professor Gordian took off down the hill with Alex close behind.

Alex was exhilarated. He skied easily and he tried a few turns. No problem! His confidence grew as he descended and he built up more and more speed. Crystals of snow gleamed in the sunlight and caught the corner of Alex's eye. He turned to survey the broad expanse of slope to his right. The beauty was breathtaking. The cold breeze on his face was intoxicating. He closed his eyes and bathed in the sensation of speed. Suddenly he heard Professor Gordian's voice calling to him. As he opened his eyes he realized that he had been daydreaming and the sudden presence of danger gave him a start. He was hurtling downward straight toward a tree! Alex was shocked into alertness and immediately and instinctively executed a jet turn, a technique that he used expertly when downhill skiing. Or he almost executed one. The Nordic equipment was just not designed for such violent techniques and Alex's feet went straight up into the air. He hit the snow at an angle and somersaulted sideways before rolling down the hill into the tree. Professor Gordian skied over and surveyed the damage.

"Are you all right?" he asked.

"Well, everything except for my pride," Alex answered with a grin.

"Ho, ho! That was quite a spill! I think that you just became a victim of *Einstellung*."

"Is that the legendary snow snake that jumps out of the snow to trip passing skiers?"

"Not exactly, but I'm sure that the snow snake is some kind of relative. Einstellung is the German word for set, and is another of the general factors that hinder problem solving. When you were confronted by the problem of the approaching tree, you attempted to solve it by performing a maneuver that you had performed many times in the past and which had worked for you then. But the situation was different now and your solution path did not work as planned."

Professor Gordian helped Alex out of the snow, and after dusting him off, they decided to rest a moment.

"Einstellung is something else that was investigated by Karl Duncker. He gave subjects a large number of problems that could all be solved in the same way. For instance, suppose that you have three jars and a water tap. Jar *A* holds 21 cups, jar *B* holds 127 cups and jar *C* holds 3 cups. The goal is to measure out 100 cups of water. What would you do?"

Alex thought a moment and answered. "Fill jar *B,* then fill jar *A* from jar *B,* then fill jar *C* from jar *B* twice. This leaves you with 100 cups in jar *B*.

"Right! Now suppose jar *A* holds 13 cups, jar *B* holds 163 cups, and jar *C* holds 25 cups. What do you do now?"

Alex reflected briefly and answered, "You could do the same thing: Fill *B,* subtract *A* and then subtract *C* twice."

"Right again. Duncker gave subjects this task several times, each problem solvable by the same method, $B - A - 2C$. Then, he gave them a problem like this. Jar *A* holds 23 cups, jar *B* holds 49 cups, and jar *C* holds 3 cups. Measure out 20 cups."

"You could do the same thing again, right?"

"Correct, and this is what Duncker's subjects did. But there is an easier way."

"Oh sure! Just fill *A* and subtract *C*! You get used to doing something one way and don't see that there is an easier way."

"All right now, Alex, just remember that there is an easier way and don't go crashing into any more trees."

They spent the rest of the afternoon exploring the mountains close to the cabin. That evening they went back to the cabin to eat and sit around the fireplace. After dinner Professor Gordian proposed a new game instead of poker.

"This is one version of a game called nim, Alex. You place fifteen pennies on the table. Each player alternates taking pennies. You can take from one to five pennies at each turn. The player who takes the last penny wins."

"That sounds like fun," said Alex. "Who goes first?"

"You go first this time" replied the professor.

"I'm sure I'll need all the advantage I can get," said Alex as he took two pennies.

"What makes you think that the first player has the advantage." asked the professor, taking one penny. "You don't think that I would let you have any advantage, do you?"

Alex concentrated on the row of pennies on the table and took three. "This appears to be a game of pure skill, and I would think that one of the players has an advantage simply by virtue of playing either first or second. Do you mean to tell me the second player has the advantage?"

Professor Gordian smiled and took three pennies. "Since you are being insistent, Alex, I will tell you that with proper play the first player will always win."

Alex raised his eyebrows and then looked at the six pennies remaining on the table. He saw that he had lost. No matter how many pennies he took, the professor would be able to remove the last penny. "You mean with proper play, quite unlike my own?"

"Well, you could stand a bit of improvement," the professor teased.

"This is a very difficult game to figure out!" said Alex with a frown. "There seem to be so many possibilities. How do you figure out what is 'proper play'? Do you have to write down all of the possible plays and choose those that lead to a win for the first player?"

"That would be one way to do it," answered the professor, "but work there is a very effective problem solving strategy that could be backwards employed here. Whenever you have a problem where the goal state is clear, but the present state is ambiguous, then it sometimes helps to try working backwards. Remember the problem yesterday with the 1025 tennis players? The goal state is very clear, one winner and 1024 losers. Now consider this. Every game has one winner and one loser, correct? Since a loser cannot go on to play another game, every loser represents one game of tennis, the one he lost. Therefore, the number of games played is the same as the number of losers, 1024."

Alex nodded his head. "That's pretty clever! Let me look at the end of a game of nim. A player will win if there are from one to five pennies left when it is his turn, because he can take them all." Alex thought for a minute. "And if your opponent has six pennies left on his last turn, you will have from one to five pennies left after he plays! So the goal is to leave your opponent with six pennies on his last turn. You can do this on the next to last turn if there are, uh, from seven to eleven pennies." Alex paused again. "And you can force your opponent to leave from seven to eleven pennies on the next to last turn if you leave your opponent with twelve on your first turn. So the first player can win by taking three pennies on his first play. Let's play again!"

Professor Gordian laughed as Alex quickly gathered the pennies and lined them up again (See Figure 7). "It certainly didn't take very long for you to figure that out!"

"It's just a matter of knowing how to approach the problem," said Alex with mock seriousness as he picked up three pennies. Professor Gordian took one penny, and Alex took five, leaving six on the table. "Ha! Got you!" taunted Alex. "Now we're even." Professor Gordian conceded.

Becoming more sedate, Alex said, "I know that a master shouldn't teach his student all he knows, but can you tell me about any other useful approaches when the going gets difficult? I

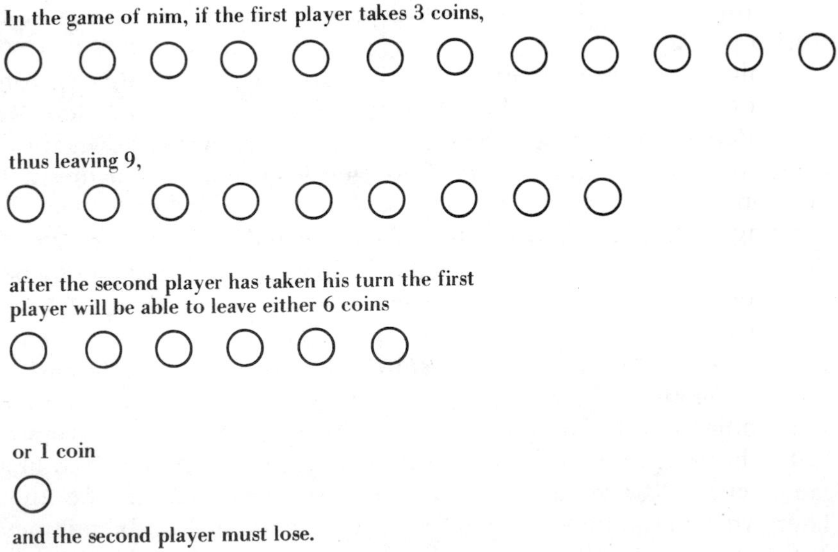

In the game of nim, if the first player takes 3 coins,

thus leaving 9,

after the second player has taken his turn the first player will be able to leave either 6 coins

or 1 coin

and the second player must lose.

Figure 7. Optimal strategy for the game of nim.

mean some tool that might apply to many different types of problems?"

"With the danger of allowing you to get the upper hand, I will tell you one more possible solution path tonight before we go to bed. When you have a problem, you will have it represented in some fashion, be it a verbal description, a diagram, mathematical equations, or some other model. It turns out that some representations are much better for some types of problems than others. So you might try changing the representation to a more appropriate form. For example, suppose you took this sheet of typing paper and folded it in half. Then suppose that you kept on folding it in half 50 times. How thick would it be after you were through? Try visualizing this." **try changing representation**

"I think that it would be very thick when I was through, but I can't imagine the process after about four or five folds. I would guess about 50 feet."

"That isn't even close, Alex. You had difficulty with this problem because visual representation breaks down here. A mathematical representation would be much more appropriate. Every time you fold the paper its thickness doubles, and so you are multiplying the original thickness of the paper by two, 50 times, or 2^{50}. This is a very large number, and the answer would be closer to half the distance to the sun!"

"Wow! Math is a very powerful tool. So you would suggest trying to put a problem into a mathematical representation whenever possible?"

"Not by any means. There is a time and place for everything and there are times when a mathematical representation would make things more complicated, not easier. Try this. A man and a woman are walking together. At this moment their right feet are striking the ground. The man takes two steps for the woman's three. How many steps does each take before their left feet strike the ground simultaneously?"

"Well this one I can see in my head (as shown in Figure 8). Their right feet are on the ground now, and then their feet don't strike simultaneously again until the man has taken two steps and the woman three. Then he has his right foot down and she has her left. Then their feet don't strike simultaneously again until another two steps by the man and three by the woman. Now his right foot is down and so is hers. Their left feet never do hit the ground together!"

"Correct. A mathematical approach wouldn't have made that

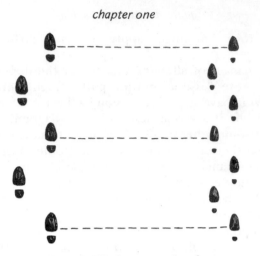

Figure 8. His feet versus her feet.

problem easier. Now give this one a try. The sum of the ages of a husband and wife is 98 years. He is twice as old as she was when he was the age she is today. What are their ages?"

"Wait a minute! I have to write this down. It sounds like a jumble of words."

After Professor Gordian had repeated the problem slowly and Alex had written it down, Professor Gordian said, "This is one of those problems where several different tools can be applied. You have used the first, writing it down. You will probably then continue by working on stable subgoals. There is an old story about two watchmakers who built watches composed of 1000 parts. The first watchmaker had to assemble all of his parts at one time without stopping, because if he left his work, the entire assembly would collapse. The other watchmaker worked by first putting together all the parts into stable substructures of ten parts each. Then he put together stable groups of ten of these and finally combined the whole thing together. I do not have to comment on who was the more successful. It helps to treat problems that way too. Try to solve various subproblems if you cannot solve the whole thing at once. Here you started by writing it down, and next you will probably want to try another representation. The problem was presented verbally, and it seems clear that this is not the best way to look at the problem."

Alex had already begun translating the problem into mathematical symbols and equations. His pencil was working furiously. After a minute, Alex looked up and asked, "He is 56 and she is 42, right?"

stable subgoals

Alex's solution of the age problem

Subgoal 1: Write it down

> The sum of the ages of a husband and wife is 98 years. He is twice as old as she was when he was the age she is today. What are their ages?

Subgoal 2: Assign symbols

H = husband's age today
W = wife's age today

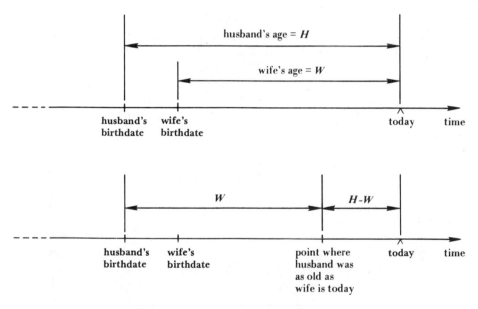

Figure 9. The husband and wife problem.

Subgoal 3: Translate into mathematical equations

$H + W = 98$
He was the age she is today $(H - W)$ years ago.
$(H - W)$ years ago she was $[W - (H - W)]$ years old.
$H = 2 [W - (W - H)]$

Subgoal 4: Solve for W

$$H = 2W - 2H + 2W$$
$$3H = 4W$$
$$H = (4/3)W$$
$$(4/3)W + W = 98$$
$$(7/3)W = 98$$
$$W = 42$$

Subgoal 5: Solve for H

$$H + 42 = 98$$
$$H = 56$$

"Right! Notice your paper and look at all the subgoals that you accomplished. Another wonderful thing about changing representation is that sometimes that in itself solves the problem instantly! You can't really divorce a problem from its mode of representation. Try this problem."

Professor Gordian drew the diagram in Figure 10 on a piece of paper. "Assume that you know the radius of the circle. Find Z in terms of the radius."

Alex immediately went to work writing equations and adding lines to the drawing. After working on the problem for about five minutes, he stopped and looked up at his uncle.

"I've got to be going about this in the wrong way. You said that the proper representation would solve it immediately. What am I doing wrong?"

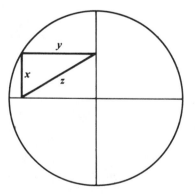

Figure 10. The circle problem.

With a sly look on his face Professor Gordian drew an additional line in the diagram as in Figure 11. "The diagonals of a rectangle are equal, are they not? So Z is equal to the other diagonal, which is the radius."

Alex sat back in his seat and slumped. "Phew! I don't think the master has to worry about this student surpassing him."

"Don't worry, Alex. Experience comes with age. One of the nice things about changing representation is that it allows you to get a new perspective on a problem. You might be very familiar with a problem but still fail to use all the information available. You might be so familiar with the problem that you think you know all the information but you do not. This is a phenomenon called saturation. As an example, you are very familiar with phone dials, having seen them hundreds of times, right? But I challenge you to draw a picture from memory alone including all of the numbers and letters in the proper positions. Artists encounter the same problem. When they attempt to draw a familiar scene, they often cannot recall how everything actually looks. A change of representation can present the familiar in a novel light so that more information can be utilized. Artists sometimes do this by looking through their legs at a scene so as to see it upside down."

saturation

Alex got up and looked at Professor Gordian through his legs. "Yes, professor, you look a lot wiser from this angle. But not a bit older."

With that they bid each other a cheery goodnight.

*   *   *   *

The next day was very cold, still, and clear. The sun shone brightly on the white snow and Alex and Professor Gordian skied away from the cabin through broad expanses of snow blanketed meadows. They had planned to go in a large loop, skirting the edge of the forest which surrounded the cabin. They skied happily for several hours and then stopped for lunch on a log resting under a large fir tree.

While they were eating Alex complained of severe pain in his eyes. "It feels as though someone has poured sand into my eyes," moaned Alex.

Professor Gordian took off Alex's sunglasses and noticed that Alex's eyes were very red. When he looked through Alex's glasses, he was immediately aware of the source of Alex's pain.

"Alex, these glasses are so light you could wear them at night! You have sunburned your eyes."

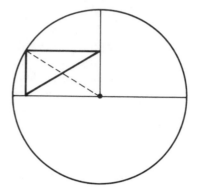

Figure 11. Change in representation in the circle problem.

"But those are the only glasses that I have. How am I going to get back to the cabin?"

"We will have to go back through the forest, where it isn't so bright. In the meantime, we will have to improve your glasses temporarily." He reached into his rucksack and pulled out some matches and a candle, supplies he always carried for emergency fire starting. As he lit the candle and started to hold Alex's glasses over the flame, Alex objected.

"Wait! The frames are plastic and they might melt!"

"I'm just going to smoke the lenses a bit to give your eyes some more protection. Do you have any other ideas?" asked the professor.

"But those glasses are very expensive!" protested Alex.

"The most important thing now is for you to be able to get back to the cabin without damaging your eyes even more. The cost of replacing these sunglasses is insignificant compared to the value of your eyesight, or even compared to a bill for one visit to a good ophthalmologist."

"I guess you're right. It's just hard to get the proper perspective on things where money is concerned. My dad has always taught me the value of taking care of my money."

world view constraints "I agree with your father, Alex. However, in this specific situation that lesson is acting as a world view constraint. That is the inability to see a situation in any way other than from one restricted, but all encompassing viewpoint. You look at your expensive glasses, and you think they must be protected. After all, you don't want to throw away money. But there comes a time when there are more important things than money. This constraint reminds me of a very brilliant friend of mine who was a mathematics professor. He was presented with a sequence of symbols and told it was very familiar to him. The sequence was 32, 38, 44, 48, 56, 60. He was asked to figure out what the next symbol in the sequence was. He spent quite a while with it, and not being able to produce a simple answer, he generated a polynomial expression to fit all the given numbers and then computed the next number in the series from the expression. He was shocked when he was told that the correct answer was 'Meadowlark.' He immediately realized where the sequence came from. Every day he went to work on the subway which stopped at 32nd St., 38th St., 44th St., 48th St., 56th St., 60th St., and finally stopped at Meadowlark Street, where he got off. He was unable to consider the symbols as representing anything but some type of mathematical relationship. A similar example is this one. What is the next letter in this sequence?" Professor Gordian took a twig and wrote the letters, B, C, D, G, J, O in the snow.

Alex studied the letters and questioningly replied, "T?"

"How did you come up with T, Alex?" asked Professor Gordian.

"Well, there are no intervening letters between B and C, nor are there any between C and D. But there are two letters between D and G, and there are two letters between G and J. Between J and O there are four letters, so I would guess that the same pattern would continue and there would be four letters between O and the next letter, which would be T."

"And what if I told you that T was incorrect and the next letter was actually P? What would you guess to be the next letter?"

"Well, there goes that idea." After studying the letters for another minute Alex cried, "Oh! Is it the shape of the letters? If you are just listing all the letters with curves, then the next letter would be a Q."

"Yes, that was my idea. Most people when presented with that problem look for some mathematical relationship between the letters, rather than looking at the form of the letters. This is natural because it is the sort of thing that is taught in school, but sometimes it's unproductive and becomes a world view constraint."

After Professor Gordian had smoked Alex's glasses the two of them made their way back through the forest to the cabin. There Alex applied cold compresses to his eyes while Professor Gordian gathered up their things and packed them into the van. The plan was for Professor Gordian to drive home while Alex lay in the back of the van with his eyes closed. After they had positioned themselves in the van, Professor Gordian tried to start the engine. When he turned the ignition key, the engine turned over depressingly slowly, sounding much like someone trying to saw through a board as slowly as possible with a dull hand saw.

"Well, Alex, what do you suggest we do?" inquired the professor.

"I think that the cold has gotten to the battery, which wasn't too strong to begin with. Before this weekend, I would have been at a loss, because of an associational constraint. But now I know exactly what to do."

Alex directed the professor to remove the battery from the car and take it into the still warm cabin.

While they were waiting for the battery to warm up, Alex inquired, "Uncle, I've learned a lot about problem solving from talking with you this weekend. But I'm afraid it has all come too quickly for me to remember everything. Could you write an outline of the things we have talked about?"

"Gladly, Alex," replied the professor.

Professor Gordian took a notebook and a pencil out of the desk drawer and thoughtfully outlined some general guides to problem solving.

After Professor Gordian had finished, he reinstalled the battery in the car and the engine started up with only a little trouble. Professor Gordian was hoping for an uneventful trip home.

The outline the professor made is given below:

SUMMARY

1/ A problem exists when "what is" is not the same as "what is desired"

2/ A model is an abstract representation of reality

3/ A model of a problem can be given as follows:

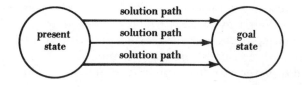

4/ Human values are implicated in the problem solving process at all stages: present state, goal state, and solution paths

5/ A model of the problem solving process can be given as:
 a/ perceive and analyze the problem components
 b/ formulate hypotheses about possible solution paths
 c/ select among hypotheses
 d/ test the most likely hypotheses
 e/ incubate if all tests fail
 (errors are possible at any of the above stages)

6/ Some common failings in problem solving include:
 a/ difficulty isolating the problem
 b/ associational constraints—constraints introduced by making inappropriate associations to problem elements
 c/ functional constraints—constraints introduced by seeing problem elements as having only their usual function
 d/ *Einstellung* (set)—tendency to repeat an already successful solution path
 e/ world view constraint—inability to see the problem from other than a restricted perspective
 f/ cultural, emotional, and environmental constraints
 g/ inability to see the problem from the viewpoints of others
 h/ failure to use all relevant information—because of limit of memory, or stereotyping, or other forms of bias
 i/ using an inappropriate representation

7/ Some general precepts in problem solving:
 a/ get the whole picture
 b/ have a will to doubt, withhold judgment
 c/ write things down
 d/ use models
 e/ ask appropriate questions
 f/ try a change of representation
 g/ explore all plausible directions

8/ Some possible solution paths:
   a/ discuss the problem—both talk and listen
   b/ use similarities with solved problems
   c/ use analogies and metaphors
   d/ use stable subgoals
   e/ try specializing or generalizing, or use induction
   f/ try the method of contradiction
   g/ try working backwards

PROBLEMS

1/ Pick a personal problem that you have and cast it into the model of a problem in general, i.e., present state, goal state, and solution paths.
   a/ describe the present state, "what is"
   b/ describe the goal state, "what is desired"
   c/ give some tentative solution paths that you might try
   d/ what might the future state be if no action is taken? (i.e., if no solution path is taken)
   e/ discuss how values enter into your formulation of this problem at the initial state, goal state, and tentative solution paths

2/ Repeat problem 1, but with a social problem instead of a personal problem. Some examples of social problems might deal with population control, pollution, treatment of criminals, distribution of wealth, etc. Discuss the values of society that could affect your approach to a solution.

3/ In looking for solutions to the problems picked in 1 and 2 above, determine how accurately the general model of the problem solving *process* in Professor Gordian's outline (item 5) describes the process that you used. If there are any discrepancies try to explain why they exist.

4/ From your own experience briefly describe an example of a problem in which arrival at an effective solution was hindered by:
   a/ difficulty in isolating the problem
   b/ an association constraint
   c/ a function constraint
   d/ a world view constraint
   e/ Einstellung
   f/ cultural, emotional, or environmental constraints
   g/ inability to see the problem from the viewpoint of others
   h/ failure to use all relevant information
   i/ using an inappropriate representation

Note: The following are problems for your enjoyment. In attempting to solve them, use the general precepts given in Professor Gordian's outline, and also try the possible solution paths listed there if you should reach an impasse.

5/ A farmer had a square property with 24 trees, as shown in Figure 12. In his will he stated that each of his 8 sons should receive the same amount of land and the same number of trees. How would you divide the land? (Can you identify any constraints under which you are operating?)

6/ How can you divide an area bounded by a circle into ten parts with only three lines? (Can you identify any constraints under which you are operating?)

7/ Many years from now, two readers of this book meet on the street. The following is part of their discussion:

Person 1: Yes, I'm married and have three fine sons.
Person 2: That's nice. How old are they?

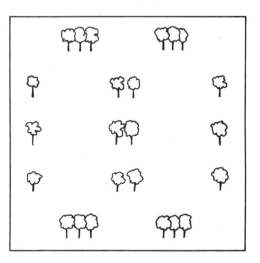

Figure 12. Map for Problem 5.

Person 1: Well, the product of their ages is equal to 36.

Person 2: Hmm. That doesn't tell me enough. Give me another clue.

Person 1: O.K. The sum of their ages is the number on the building across the street.

Person 2: (After a few minutes of thinking with the aid of pencil and paper): Ah ha! I've almost got the answer, but I still need another clue.

Person 1: Very well. The oldest one has red hair.

Person 2: I've got it!

What were the ages of the three sons of Person 1? (Hint: All ages are integers. Try writing things down, use stable subgoals, use models, and get the whole picture.)

8/ A room is 30 feet long, 12 feet high, and 12 feet wide. A fly with a broken wing is standing on one of the short walls 1 foot from the ceiling and 6 feet from each corner. A sticky fingered child has just smeared jelly from a peanut butter and jelly sandwich on the opposite wall 1 foot from the floor and 6 feet from each corner. What is the shortest path the fly could take to walk to the jelly smear? (Hint: Try a change of representation.)

9/ In the "Tower of Hanoi" game, eight discs rest on pin 1, as shown in Figure 13. What is the minimum number of steps required to move the eight

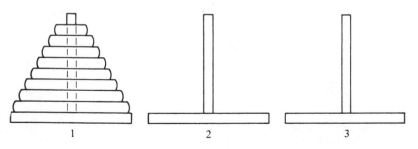

Figure 13. The "Tower of Hanoi" game

discs to either pin 2 or pin 3? A step is defined as movement of one disc from one pin to another. You can remove only one disc at a time, and a larger disc can never rest on top of a smaller disc. (Hint: Try using stable subgoals, specialization, and generalization.)

10/ Through some misadventure, a cat fell down a well which was eight feet deep. The cat managed to climb out, but only after experiencing great difficulty. Every day he would climb up three feet, but he would fall back two feet during the night. How long did it take the cat to get out of the well? (You may assume that the day and night are 12 hours long each. Hint: Try using generalization or specialization, but be careful.)

11/ Five friends named Jones, Stacey, Young, Lewis, and Smith were involved in a battle and one of the men was killed. The following facts are known:

a/ Jones was an ordained Catholic priest.

b/ The wife of the slain man was the sister of Mrs. Lewis.

c/ Mrs. Smith's beautiful daughter died of infantile paralysis.

d/ Stacey was sorry that Young did not return on the same boat with him.

e/ Mrs. Lewis regretted that she never had a niece or nephew.

Which man was killed in the battle? (Hint: Try using the method of contradiction.)

12/ A horse trader brings a string of horses to a horse fair. As admission charge, he gives up one of his horses. At the fair he sells one half of those remaining, and on the way out he is charged one horse as a trading fee. He proceeds to a second fair where similar conditions prevail. There he pays one horse to get in, sells half of the horses he still has on hand, and pays a single horse as a trading fee. Not content he proceeds to a third fair. Here again he pays one horse to get in, sells one half of the horses remaining, and is charged a single horse on the way out as a trading fee. He then has one horse left which he rides home with his proceeds. How many horses did he start out with? (Hint: Try working backwards.)

13/ Given a five by five checkerboard, as shown in Figure 14, try to draw a line through all the squares of the checkerboard, starting from the square with the dot in it on the left side and passing through each box once and only once, without lifting the pencil from the paper, without ever passing outside the checkerboard, and without drawing diagonal lines. Show how to do it, or prove it impossible. (Hint: Have you seen a similar problem?)

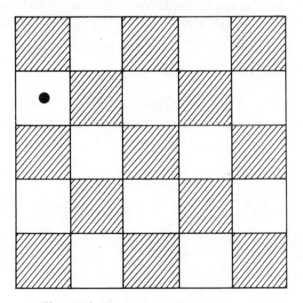

Figure 14. Checkerboard for Problem 13.

PROJECT

Pick a problem of broad reaching social consequence. Cast it into a present state, goal state, and solution path model. Describe in detail the present state, future state if no action is taken, and the goal state. Make a list of possible solution paths. Try to withhold judgment and make an extensive, even if not entirely practical, list. Are you operating under any constraints? Try to identify them. Discuss the problem with a friend, and try to increase the length of your list of possible solution paths. Now narrow down your list to the most practical alternatives. Use any of the relevant guides discussed in this chapter to help you arrive at a solution. Identify the important values you are using in the formulation of your problem and in choosing solution paths.

2

Languages, Models, and Modeling

Alex was sprawled on a park bench, shaking with paroxysms of laughter. A daily newspaper dangled from his limp hand as he gasped for air between his convulsions of hilarity.

"Alex! What are you so cracked up about?" came a voice from the distance.

Alex controlled his laughter for long enough to glance up to see Professor Gordian striding down the walk toward him. "Oh hi, Professor!" Alex managed to squeeze in a greeting between gasps.

Professor Gordian approached the bench and Alex struggled to sit up to make room for his uncle. As the Professor sat down, Alex tried to explain his source of mirth. "I was just reading about this woman who was shot." Professor Gordian's eyes widened in obvious amazement. "Oh, that's not what is so funny. In fact, the story is not funny at all. On the contrary, it is tragic. But the way the story is reported is just amazing. Apparently a man became angered at his wife because of some sort of marital conflict. To make a long story short he ended up shooting her. The bullet entered her head but did not kill her. When she arrived at the hospital the doctors decided that they must not operate at once to remove the bullet because of possible complications. What struck me funny was the caption of the article." Alex showed his uncle the headline. It read "Man shoots wife in head, bullet is in her still."

Alex again chuckled. "When I first saw that, I conjured up this picture of a man shooting a woman in the bathroom and the bullet going through her and lodging in a liquor still that they were using to make bootleg whiskey. I had to read the article to make sure that my first idea was not right!"

Professor Gordian laughed. "That's a pretty funny example of ambiguity of how ambiguous our natural language of English can be. It reminds me of another example you would probably enjoy. I heard my wife the other day talking on the phone to one of her friends. I was not listening to all of the conversation, but one comment she made attracted my attention. She said 'The shooting of the hunters was terrible!' At one and the same time a picture of clumsy nimrods competed in my mind with a picture of some murderous act perpetrated on a group of hunters by gangsters. I had to question her later to find out what she was talking about. It's amazing how ambiguous our language can really be."

Alex looked thoughtful. "You know, I was just thinking the same thing. A friend of mine, who is pretty much of a nut, told me about a game he used to play. He would engage in conversations, or just listen to other people talking, and he would try to find as many ambiguous meanings as possible. He could make a pun out of nearly every other sentence! I tried it myself and I could do the same thing. It was an amusing pastime, but I ended up driving all of my friends crazy. So I quit, before I was involuntarily committed."

Alex smiled, as he embarrassedly recalled the playful antics of youth. A more serious expression returned to his face and he became contemplative. "You know, Professor, it really is a wonder that people can understand each other at all. Given the ambiguity of language, and the mere fact that we can pervert the meaning of nearly every sentence, it is curious why communication usually seems so easy."

The Professor nodded his head knowingly. "I think that language is normally an efficient means of communication because usually there is some context in which utterances are embedded. The context determines, or helps determine, a fairly unique meaning. For example, if you were walking down the street in the middle of a large city and you saw a sign in a window that said 'We sell alligator shoes' you would probably not mistake its meaning. Seldom do people buy shoes for their pet alligators! Notice that where the context is not so clearly delimiting, however, a sentence

(margin notes:) ambiguity of natural language

communication and context

can still be ambiguous. If you were walking downtown and you saw a sign in a store window that read 'We sell horseshoes' it would probably not arouse much uncertainty as to its meaning. If, however, you were walking down a street in a small country town and saw the same sign in a general store window, you might begin to wonder exactly what the sign was advertising.

"Also, not only does the context of the physical environment aid understanding, but one can usually deduce a person's intention from his voice's inflection and intonation, as well as from non-verbal communication, or body language. There are quite a few factors that help us to understand the spoken and written word. In addition to these factors, language is also highly redundant. In most cases language provides much more information than is needed to transmit a message. As an example, you can write a sentence and omit all of the articles and the sentence will usually still be intelligible. In fact, you can even write a sentence and omit all of the vowels and it will remain intelligible in most cases. Try this."

inflection, intonation, body language

redundancy

Professor Gordian reached over, took the newspaper and wrote in the margin, "Mst ppl cn rd ths sttmnt with lttl dffclty."

Alex looked over at the paper and laughed. "Ho! That's great! I haven't really thought about the redundancy of language. To me, the difficulties in communication seem so overwhelming. I guess a major reason for this is because I spend so much time at school in the classroom. In everyday conversation it is easy to see how context and redundance allow facile communication. But in the classroom, especially in math or science or philosophy classrooms, the shortcomings of language are striking. I will listen to the teacher talking about some subject, and sometimes I just can not grasp what he is trying to put across. And there are other times when I think I understand, and the next sentence or two convinces me that I had not really understood at all. When talking about very complex or abstract or novel subjects, the faults of language become glaring."

"I agree with you Alex. I have the same problem in the classroom, only from the other end. I find it extremely difficult at times to put my thoughts into words, and particularly to put my thoughts into words that my students can understand. In order to understand something, you have to be able to relate it to something that you already know. But in the case of novel or abstract subjects, it is sometimes very difficult to find something that students can relate the new ideas to. It's hard to find an appropriate context in the absence of a common frame of reference. People

understanding

43

have different experiences, and words mean different things to different people."

TUCKER   by Joe Martin

Figure 15. Courtesy Field Syndicate, Inc.

"That's an interesting way of putting it, Professor. I suppose that you don't have the same order of magnitude of problems when you are communicating with colleagues, because there is more likely a common frame of reference."

"That's true, but that is not to say that there are never any problems. There are quite often misunderstandings among professionals about just what someone is trying to say. In fact, this difficulty sometimes turns out to be an asset. Some of the greatest scientific discoveries in history have been made by someone interpreting someone else's statements about the world in a manner other than the intended one. For example, Einstein looked at the notion of time in a different light than had previously been seriously considered, and came up with the theory of special relativity."

Alex thought over what the Professor had said. "It seems that man, with all his amazing conquests, would have come up with a better means of communication than the languages he now uses. It would seem that there should be a less ambiguous means of expression."

"Well, in fact, there are systems of representation that are much more precise in some ways than natural language. Remember that natural language is just another example of a model, although it is an all pervasive one. Language is a representation for reality and for thought, although some people would say that at least part of thinking is language. But as with all models or systems of representation, there are possible alternatives. Symbolic logic is one such alternative. Systems of logic have been devised to overcome ambiguity in natural language. Systems of logic define very precisely the meaning of certain expressions and logical connectors such as 'and,' 'some,' 'if-then,' and so on. Logic deals with truth

logic

truth values

44

values. If simple statements are known to be either true or false, then logic can determine whether compound statements involving the original simple statements are true or false. There can be no errors of ambiguity in this system, because the meaning of the terms involved is *defined* by their truth values. For example, suppose you have two simple statements, say 'I am a man' and 'I am 50 years old.' If both of these statements are true, then the compound statement 'I am a man and I am 50 years old' must be true. If either simple statement is false, then the compound statement must be false. The meaning of 'and' can thus be defined in terms of these truth values. This is a fine system, and newer and more sophisticated systems are continually being devised to deal with more general and more complex problems. But logic is not an end in itself. By restricting itself to a formal system of symbols in which there is no ambiguity, logic lacks something. It lacks the richness of meaning that is characteristic of natural language. It lacks the fertility of natural language that cultivates creative new ideas. And logic is restricted in the sense that it relies on human, subjective criteria for the initial assignment of truth values to statements. Thus, it is a system for manipulating thoughts and ideas that have already been linked with reality by means of less precise methods."

disadvantages of logic

"I think I understand what you are saying," said Alex, "because I have had some exposure to logic in math classes. Logic itself is a model for reality, and it has very precise rules for manipulating elements within the model. The truth or falseness of any element in the model can be determined precisely, without ambiguity or error, if some elements in the model are given an initial truth assignment from outside the model. What is lacking in logic is some unambiguous means for getting from reality to the model. The initial truth assignments can be faulty, and this will influence the truth values of the conclusions reached by the model. This reminds me of mathematics, where you have a formal, logical system, but which says nothing about how the elements in the system are related to the real world. You have a complete abstraction."

logic as a model

"Right you are," said Professor Gordian. "Let me give you a simple example in logic. Take this argument. The first premise is that all poisonous things are bitter. The second premise is that arsenic is not bitter. If these first two premises are true, then it must follow from the meaning of the words involved that arsenic is not poisonous. But everyone knows better than that! The conclusion is false, because the first premise is false. But this is not the fault of logic. It is the fault of accepting the truth of the premises.

45

The rules of logic deal with the validity of a conclusion derived from premises whose truth or falseness is assumed."

models are not reality

"I see," said Alex. "So logic is just another model, another tool for thinking and decision making. It is not reality."

models are tools for understanding and prediction

"True," replied Professor Gordian. "People often have the problem that they mistake models for reality. They don't realize that a model is just a tool for understanding and prediction. The fact that models are not reality is obvious in some cases, but somewhat less obvious in others. Take, for example, a model that Freud postulated to try to understand human behavior. He felt that personality was made up of three different components: the id, the ego, and the superego. He conceived of the id as being a repository for instinctual energy concerned with directly satisfying basic hedonistic drives, like hunger and sex. The superego represents the influences of socialization by the parents. It is concerned with morality and guilt. The ego is the executive branch of personality. It guides the person through physical reality, satisfying at the same time the hedonistic strivings of the id and the moralistic urgings of the superego, and rationally dealing with reality all the time. Freud formulated an analogy to help explain the workings of the psyche. He conceived of the ego as being a charioteer trying to control two powerful, unruly horses trying to pull in opposite directions. The charioteer must coordinate the conflicting strivings of the two horses and guide the chariot down the road without going off into a ditch. This chariot analogy is quite obviously a model, as it is clear there are no chariots and horses in our minds directing our thinking. But what is not quite so obvious is that the entire system of id, superego, and ego is also a model. Id, superego,

hypothetical constructs

and ego are hypothetical constructs, postulated to try to explain and predict human behavior. We cannot physically identify anything corresponding to the id or the other personality components. They have no direct sensory components; they cannot be seen, heard, smelled, touched, or tasted.

"While most people avoid confusing such psychological or other social science models with reality, many people just cannot resist the temptation to confuse models of physics with reality. Physical constructs like gravity, magnetism, electricity, atoms, or quarks are merely models for the way the world behaves. These constructs are inferred from observable events in the world. We commonly say that phenomena occur because of these constructs. For example, one might say that this pencil drops to the ground when I release it in mid air 'because' of gravity. What is often forgotten is that gravity is a mental construct, inferred from observations that objects usually do fall to the ground when released. We can use the construct of gravity to explain many diverse phenomena. Many people end up thinking that there is some physical thing called gravity which lawfully determines how objects behave in the world. They lose sight of the fact that gravity has been created in the minds of men and is in fact nothing more than a model for the way things behave in reality. A simple consideration that should convince anyone of this point is to notice how models of physics have changed historically. For example, Democritus first postulated the atom as the building block of all matter. He considered the atom to be indivisible. Then man increased the sophistication of the concept of the atom by dividing it into electrons and protons. Then came neutrons, positrons, neutrinos, mesons, quarks, and a whole host of new conceptualizations. These new ideas have had to be invented in order to account for the discovery of knowledge that could not be explained by the older models.

"As a specific example of how physical models change with the discovery of new information, consider the fate of the electron particle theory. Neils Bohr postulated a model of the atom that was very much like the solar system. It had a central nucleus around which electrons revolved, like the planets revolve around the sun. The electron was conceived to be a discrete particle. In all investigations up until Bohr created his model, the electron had been observed to behave like a particle. If you take a thin sheet of plastic and put a small pin hole in it and beam electrons through the hole onto a photographic plate, you will get a circular exposure pattern on the plate where the electrons have impacted. The model of the electron as a miniscule particle had been supported by this experiment and many others. But then new evidence was discovered that was inconsistent with the interpretation of the electron as a particle. If you put two holes in the sheet before beaming electrons through them, the particle model would predict that you will get two circular patterns of light on the photographic plate. But when you actually perform this experiment you get alternating bands of light and dark instead! Something must be wrong. The electrons are behaving like waves, reinforcing and canceling each other. You can get the same effect by playing in your bathtub if you make a cardboard barrier with two slots. Making waves behind the barrier produces diverging wave patterns on the other side of the barrier. These patterns interfere to produce alternating areas of high and low waves at the edge of the tub. The fact that electrons have wave properties made it necessary to modify our conception of an electron as a particle." The experiment is shown in Figure 16.

models
approximate
physical
reality, but
are not
'truth' "Our models change to provide us with better and better approximations to the way the world behaves. Our models approximate physical reality, but the models themselves are never 'truth.' To conclude that any given model is the truth and will never need to be modified would be an incredibly egotistical presumption, since attempts of the future will always be able to uncover new knowledge. Good models are constantly changing and evolving to account for the discovery of new knowledge. But it is our knowledge and ideas as conceptualized by the models that are changing, not the world around us."

"I understand what you're saying, Professor. All through school I was told that the world behaves as it does *because* of the laws of physics, when in effect the laws of physics are just models—descriptions for what it is that we observe. It is very difficult not to regard the models of physics as physical realities when even our teachers do so."

Professor Gordian nodded his agreement. Alex spoke again after a pause. "What about really general models? I mean, models that seem to explain everything? You mentioned that models had to be modified and changed to account for the discovery of new information. But I can think of models that would be able to explain any sort of new information that might be discovered without being modified in any way. Aren't models like these more real or true than other models?"

Professor Gordian furrowed his brow. "I'm not familiar with models such as the ones you are describing. What in particular did you have in mind?"

Alex said, "Well, the model that comes into my mind first is religion. I'm not quite sure whether or not I should call it a model, since many religious sects tend to regard their religion as reality and truth, both historically and conceptually. But many religions seem to be belief systems that can explain everything. One can understand birth, death, creation, origin of species, and the nature of all events by some religious system or another. I don't see how religious models would ever have to be changed to account for new information, since religious systems can generally explain anything, without any modification necessary."

scientific
models Professor Gordian leaned forward as he spoke, "Ah, but I have been talking about *scientific* models. Religion, if you conceive of

Effect of exposing photographic plate with electrons through a pinhole:

thin barrier
with pinhole

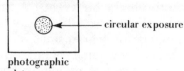

circular exposure

photographic
plate

Predicted effect of exposing photographic plate through two pinholes·

Actual effect of exposing photographic plate through two pinholes:

alternate bands of
light and dark

Wave analogy in bathtub:

splash

waves reinforce
each other here

and cancel each other here:

barrier with two slots

Figure 16. The electron experiment.

it as a model, is not a scientific model and hence cannot be judged by scientific criteria. The hallmark of a scientific model is that it refers to observable events. A scientific model, if it is to be a useful model, can be falsified by observing empirical, or observable phenomena. Religion, since it speaks of unobservables, cannot be falsified in the same manner as a scientific model. This is not to say that religion is wrong, or bad—not at all. It is just to say that religion and science are not talking about the same thing. People often get into arguments over the correctness of science versus religion. An example is the argument of evolution versus creation. I don't think that these arguments are really meaningful, since the criteria for scientific truth and religious truth are not the same. The scientist refers to observable, falsifiable phenomena, while the religious person refers to subjective beliefs based on faith. The scientific and the religious are speaking different languages."

Alex sat back and cocked his head to one side. "Yes, I remember from a class in philosophy that I took last year that science only investigates phenomena that are observable and public—that is, things that can be observed by anyone, and where the contents of the observation can be agreed upon by the observers. I think there was one other criterion for a scientific observation. . ."

criteria for scientific observation

"The three criteria for scientific observation are that the phenomena must be *observable, public,* and *repeatable,*" Professor Gordian piped in, "The public criterion rules out of the scientific domain any subjective phenomena that can only be observed by one person. It is still possible to scientifically investigate some mental phenomena by self report, however. You can have a person tell you what is going on in his head, and that report is public. Psychologists often investigate mental processes, but only in terms of the reports or behavior of subjects. Observing your own mental processes is not scientific, because it is not public. But you can scientifically verify the contents of your own subjective observations by investigating verbal reports of other people.

"The criterion of repeatability insures that science can only investigate reliable phenomena that can be repeated and verified. This rules out events like the investigation of one-time occurrences, such as someone having a mystic or psychic vision. If these events are repeatable, then they can be investigated scientifically. For example, some people claim to be able to guess the identity of cards hidden from their view. If they can repeatably and reliably do this more accurately than what can be expected on the basis of chance alone, then the phenomena can be studied scientifically. But if a person claims awareness of the death of a loved one before being informed of the event in any conventional fashion, and if the person claims that this was the only time in their lives that they have ever had such an experience, then this cannot be investigated scientifically. The event falls into the domain of the mystical, the religious, or the subjective."

"So," Alex said, "the controversy between scientists and mystics is not really meaningful. The scientist voluntarily restricts not only what can fall into his domain of investigation, but how it can be investigated, while the mystic is not so restricted."

"Yes, that is the way I see it, anyway. I am sure there are people who do not agree with me. And it is a good thing, too! Everyone would be bored stiff with nothing to argue about."

Alex and the Professor chuckled together. When their mirth subsided, Alex asked, "Are there any scientific models that are so general that they can explain everything?"

"Well, yes and no, Alex. It depends on whose point of view you take. There are some models put forth by scientists who claim that their models are scientific, and in fact it seems on the surface that these models deal with observable, public, and repeatable phenomena. But a closer look belies this initial impression. Sometimes these models are so vaguely worded and formulated that it is impossible to make any testable predictions from them. The models appear to be able to explain everything, *post hoc,* but they cannot make a definite prediction. If a definite prediction cannot be made, then a model cannot be shown to be incorrect, and hence cannot be improved. Such a model is not very useful and is an example of what I would call a pseudoscientific model. A favorite example of mine is astrology. Astrological predictions are generally worded in a vague, ambiguous fashion so that no concrete testable predictions can be made. Let me show you. Look up your daily horoscope in the paper."

good models
are falsifiable

Alex turned to the horoscope section and read his daily prediction. "It says that I am going to run into some money in the near future. Hey! That's good! I'm broke and could use some extra cash."

"Good for you, Alex. But why don't you try to test that prediction? If you do run into some money in the near future, then the horoscope is correct. And if you don't, then the prediction is wrong. Now why don't you consider what types of evidence would confirm the prediction?"

"Hopefully," Alex stated smugly, "I will get a huge inheritance from the estate of some elderly gentleman I had helped in my youth by lending a dime for him to make an emergency phone call."

"That would be nice, but it would be just as confirming if you found a penny in the street, or a friend returned a dollar that he had borrowed yesterday, or even if you got your paycheck this week. In fact, it would even be confirmed if you got involved in a traffic accident with a loaded armored car! It is impossible for anyone to claim that the prediction is wrong, because it is so vaguely and ambiguously worded that someone could claim an overlooked event provided the confirming evidence. Since the horoscope makes no concrete, falsifiable prediction, it is impossible to show that it is wrong. It is not a very useful model because it does not tell you very much.

"The same sorts of criticisms have been leveled at other models within the domain of legitimate science. For example, some of the critics of Freud have charged that his model of personality is too general and vaguely worded to allow testable predictions. They claim that the model is useless. It cannot be tested, and hence cannot be improved. They claim it is not even good for making predictions for practical purposes, such as telling you what sort of a personality will result from various mistakes in child rearing. I think some of these critics are going too far, since some parts of Freud's theory do allow precise prediction, and when tested, have usually been shown to be correct. But there are many parts of the theory that defy testing."

Alex tried to sum up his understanding. "So scientific models deal with observable, public, and repeatable phenomena, and good or useful scientific models are testable or falsifiable."

"Yes," agreed Professor Gordian, "that is an excellent description."

Alex and his uncle spent the next hour chatting and discussing some news items in the paper. As lunch time approached Alex started paging through the food section and drooling over the pictures. His eyes drifted to a column that offered a dinner plan, with several alternatives for each course."

"Boy, Professor, look at these recipes! They sure look good. Just think, how would cole slaw and chicken and apple pie go right now? Or how about fruit salad and meat loaf and pudding. Or potato salad and corned beef and. . ."

"Stop!" exhorted Professor Gordian. "I'm too hungry to start thinking about food right now. You must be hungry, too, the way you are ogling all of those recipes."

"I sure am hungry, and looking at these recipes isn't making me any fuller," replied Alex. "How about lunch at the snack shop?"

"Good idea!" replied the Professor, and off they went to the nearby restaurant.

On the way, Alex spoke to his uncle. "The food section lists three different types of salads, four main courses, and two desserts. Looking at all of them together I can't decide what combination sounds best. There are so many combinations, I can't even think of them all at once. I wish there was a way to list all of the possible combinations, without forgetting any, so I could imagine how each of them would go together. I might be able to decide what to get Mom to cook for dinner."

"Why don't you try a tree diagram?" asked the Professor.

"Well, I'll try it, but I don't know if my mom knows how to cook those," replied Alex in mock seriousness.

The Professor raised his eyes to the heavens. "One thing you should not ask her to cook is corn. You have plenty of that."

Alex chuckled. "OK, so what is a tree diagram?"   tree diagram

"A tree diagram is a very useful model that can be used whenever you want to enumerate or organize a combination of possible objects or events. It is one of the most useful and general models that I know of. Let me give you a simple example." Professor Gordian pulled two coins from his pocket, a nickel and a dime. "Suppose I flip both of these coins and record the outcome in terms of whether heads or tails shows up. How many possible outcomes are there?"

"Three," Alex answered quickly, "Two heads, a head and a tail, and two tails."

"That would be true if you aggregate the outcome of a head on the dime and a tail on the nickel with the outcome of a head on the nickel and a tail on the dime. But since these are distinct outcomes, there are actually four possible outcomes. Here is a tree diagram to show them all."

Professor Gordian took another corner of the newspaper and sketched out the tree diagram shown in Figure 17. "There are two events you are interested in, flipping a nickel and flipping a dime. Let's say that the first event is flipping the nickel, although it is arbitrary which we pick first. There are two possible outcomes for this event—getting a head or getting a tail. Now consider the

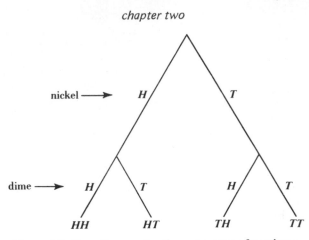

Figure 17. Tree diagram for the outcomes of tossing a nickel and a dime.

second event of flipping a dime. You can get a head or a tail on the dime, and there will be these two possible outcomes regardless of what happens with the nickel. Therefore you show these two outcomes branching from the ends of each of the possible outcomes of the first event. Now you can look down the branches of the tree diagram to see each of the four possible outcomes. Starting on the extreme left, you can get a head on the nickel and a head on the dime, a head on the nickel and a tail on the dime, a tail on the nickel and a head on the dime, and finally a tail on the nickel and a tail on the dime."

Alex looked at the paper approvingly. "Very logical and orderly. Let me try with the possible meal plans. There will be three courses, salad, main course, and dessert. For salad there can be cole slaw, fruit, and potato. For main course there can be chicken, meat loaf, corned beef, or fish. For dessert there can be apple pie or pudding. Let's see now . . . to generate a tree, first I will pick a course, which is one of salad, main course, dessert. . ."

"Now wait a minute, Alex," the Professor interrupted. "You are making a very common error for people who first try this. The levels of the tree must represent events. It is within each event that you must make a choice. All of the events occur, and you must make a choice for each event. In your problem you have three events: a salad, a main course, and a dessert. In each of these events you must make a choice. If you try to solve the problem as you have started it you will wind up at a dead end."

"I see what you mean, Professor. I must select one thing from each course, not select a course. Logically, I should start the tree with the first course—salad."

Alex sketched out the tree in Figure 18. When he finished, he contemplated the twenty four possible combinations he had enumerated. "I think I like cole slaw, chicken, and apple pie best," said Alex. When they got to the snack shop, that is what he ordered for lunch.

While they were eating, Alex was reading about a very controversial trial that was going on. Alex asked his uncle what he thought about the trial. The case involved a man who was suspected of committing a murder. Among the evidence against him was some seemingly very strong circumstantial evidence. The victim was found in a muddy area, and in the mud were footprints that were the same size as the shoes that the suspect wears. In addition, there was a piece of fabric in the victim's hand that apparently matched a hole in the suspect's jacket.

"This evidence seems pretty strong, don't you think, Professor?"

"That's an interesting question, Alex. I don't think that you can divorce the strength of evidence from the context in which it is given, so it is important to examine the context in this particular case. You can see in the paper the different strategies of the defense attorney and the prosecutor. The defense attorney is attempting to show that the evidence against his client is not very strong by demonstrating that there are a lot of people around who could have left the same evidence. The prosecutor is trying to show that the evidence is unique to the suspect—there is no one else who could have left the evidence at the scene of the crime. A good way to conceptualize the situation is with a Venn diagram."

"Hey," Alex interrupted, "I know about Venn diagrams. We **Venn** were just talking about them in a class the other day. Isn't a Venn **diagram** diagram a model that is useful for visualizing sets?"

"That's right. A set is any well-defined collection of objects or **set** events, and that is what we are talking about in this trial. We have the set of all people in the county, the set of all people who could possibly have left the footprints in the mud, the set of all people who could possibly have left the torn bit of fabric in the victim's hand, and we have the set of one person who is the murderer."

Professor Gordian turned his napkin over and proceeded to draw a Venn diagram. He started by drawing a box that represented all of the people in the county. Inside of this box, he drew a point that represented the murderer. Around this point he drew a circle that represented all of the people who could have left the footprints at the scene of the crime.

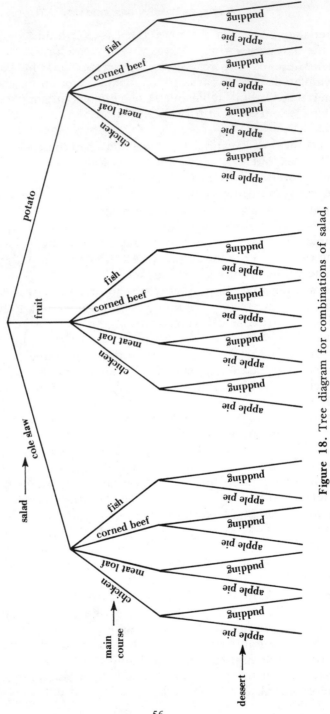

Figure 18. Tree diagram for combinations of salad, main course, and desert.

"Notice, Alex, that the points in the Venn diagram represent individual persons. When I draw a circle, I am representing a number of people. Here, all of the points in this circle are people who have the same size shoes as the murderer. The point representing the murderer falls into this circle because the murderer must have this kind of shoes. The suspect also falls into this circle because he too has the same size shoes. The question is whether the suspect and the murderer are one and the same person. What the defense attorney is going to try to do is to show that there are very many people in this circle besides the suspect. The suspect falls into this circle, and the smaller the number of people in the circle, the more likely it is that the suspect is the murderer. The prosecutor will try to show that there is no one else in the circle but the suspect. For example, if the suspect has size 15 shoes, and there is no one else in the county that has such large shoes, then it seems very likely that the suspect is the murderer. But if the suspect wears size nine shoes, which is a very common size, then the evidence is very weak. There are many other people in the circle besides the suspect.

"The other bit of evidence is the piece of fabric. I will represent this with another circle intersecting the first one. Everyone in this circle is someone who could have left the piece of fabric in the victim's hand. Notice that only a part of this circle intersects the other circle. That is because there are some people who could have left the fabric but who have the wrong size shoes, and there are some people who have the right size shoes but who could not have left the fabric. The area enclosed in both circles represents people who have the right size shoes and who could have left the fabric. These are the people we are most interested in. Just as the prosecutor will try to show that there are very few people who could have left the footprints, he will also try to show that there are very few people who could have left the fabric. He will then attempt to demonstrate that to have left the fabric and the footprints at the same time is an ability unique to the suspect. The defense attorney will try to show the opposite—that the evidence is very commonplace.

"As an example of what I have been talking about, the defense attorney might try to show that there is a club in town whose members wear jackets made out of the same material found in the victim's hand. Furthermore, since these club members frequently get into brawls, it is not unusual to find these jackets with pieces of material missing from them. And if the footprints at the scene of the crime are big, the defense attorney might point out that many people in this club are big. He will try to show that the intersection of the two circles of evidence is large, and that his client is not unique. The prosecutor will try to show that the intersection is small, and that the only possible person who could have left the evidence is the suspect, and he is thus the murderer." These Venn diagrams are all shown in Figure 19.

"That is an interesting analysis," said Alex. I hadn't analyzed the situation in nearly as much depth. It just seemed to me that the evidence was pretty incriminating. I am glad you pointed out to me the pitfalls in my thinking. Venn diagrams really help."

"Yes, I think they do too," commented his uncle. "The Venn diagram is another example of a generally useful model. It can help you solve a wide variety of different problems by helping you organize your thinking."

Alex looked impressed. "Can you give me another example of how a Venn diagram can help me solve problems?"

"I sure can, replied the Professor. "I was just noticing in the editorials section a letter written by a man who is trying to make a point about welfare. Look at this argument."

Professor Gordian underlined a paragraph in the paper. Alex read aloud. "It is clear that all those who are concerned about the disabled, the untrained, and the unemployable are in favor of some form of welfare. Since all liberals are in favor of some form of welfare, we can conclude that all those who are concerned about the disabled, the untrained, and the unemployable are liberals."

Alex's eyes opened widely as he scanned and rescanned the paragraph. "That's quite a mouthful—and a mind full," he stated in semiconfusion.

"Does that argument make sense?" asked his uncle. "Is it logically valid in the sense that if the premises are true then the conclusion must necessarily also be true?"

"Gee," said Alex, "I don't know. It is too confusing for me to figure out right away. Is there a way to use a Venn diagram to help?"

His uncle was already starting to draw a Venn diagram on the napkin. "Yes, Alex, a Venn diagram will help a lot. Look here."

Professor Gordian drew a circle in the initial box of the Venn diagram. "Let this circle represent those who are concerned about the disabled, the untrained, and the unemployable. We'll label the circle C so we don't forget. One of the premises is that everyone in this circle is in favor of some form of welfare. If I draw another

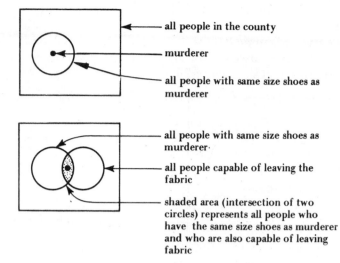

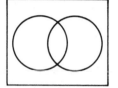

defense attorney will try to show evidence is commonplace. .

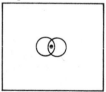

prosecutor will try to show evidence is rare, and unique to suspect. .

Figure 19. Venn diagrams for murder evidence.

circle to represent all of the people who are in favor of welfare, where should I draw it?"

Alex thought for a minute and then picked up the pencil and drew another circle surrounding the original circle. "If I draw it this way," Alex said, "then everyone in *C* is also in favor of welfare. Right?"

"Correct," responded his uncle. "Now label the circle *W* so we remember what it represents. The next premise is that all liberals

are in favor of some form of welfare. If we make a circle to represent liberals, where should we draw it?"

Alex answered immediately. "It should also go inside *W*." But I
can draw it inside *C* also, or overlapping *C*, or entirely outside of *C*.
Which is correct?" (See Figure 20.)

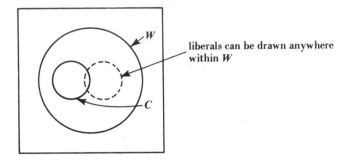

liberals can be drawn anywhere
within *W*

Figure 20. Venn diagram for argument.

"All of them may be correct, Alex, since there is no information
given to determine the exact location of the liberals. But now look
at the conclusion. It says that all who are concerned about the disabled, the untrained, and the unemployable, are liberals. That is to
say that all *C*'s are liberals. This conclusion would follow logically
if you had to draw your circle for liberals around *C*. But you do
not have to do this. The premises of the argument do not give you
sufficient reason to draw liberals surrounding *C*, so the conclusion
does not follow from the premises. You can draw liberals inside of
W but not intersecting *C*, and then the conclusion is false. Since it
is possible for the conclusion to be false when the premises are
true, the argument is not valid. A valid argument is one in which
the truth of the conclusion is insured by the truth of the premises.
That is not so here."

"So the argument is not logical!" exclaimed Alex. "It is not
easy to see that, until you organize the information in a Venn diagram. I'm excited!"

Alex went scrambling through the editorial section of the paper
looking for more arguments to check.

Later that day Alex went home and pulled out the loose leaf
"intellectual diary" that he used to record important bits of information that he collected from day to day. In this diary he carefully
summarized the things he had learned earlier that day from his
uncle:

SUMMARY

1/ Natural language is ambiguous. This is both a disadvantage and an occasional advantage. It is a disadvantage because ambiguity reduces the precision of thought and communication. Ambiguity can be an advantage when it allows for individual, subjective interpretation of theories and subsequent enrichment of understanding. Much of the ambiguity of natural language is overcome because meaning is conveyed by context, intonation and inflection, nonverbal cues, and because natural language is redundant.

2/ Symbolic logic is one means of circumventing the problem of ambiguity in natural language. Logic is a type of language in which the meaning of the elements employed is determined in a precise manner, using truth values. Given the truth or falseness of the premises, any inferences made within the model are unambiguously true or false. But ambiguity can arise due to the interpretation of the elements outside of the system, and the subsequent question of the truth or falseness of the premises in the real world.

3/ Models are abstract representations of reality, and are created in our minds. Models are not reality, but are a means for understanding and predicting what will happen in the real world. Scientific models deal with events that are observable, public, and repeatable. Good scientific models are testable and thus falsifiable, and change over time in order to become consistent with newly discovered information.

4/ Tree diagrams are useful models for enumerating combinations of outcomes of several different events. Each event is represented by one level of the tree, and each level contains all of the possible outcomes of that event.

5/ Venn diagrams are useful models for conceptualizing operations on sets. Sets are well defined collections of objects or events. Venn diagrams can be used to check inferences and arguments, as well as to aid general understanding of sets and their interrelationships.

PROBLEMS

1/ From your own experience, give an example of some of the difficulties in using natural language to communicate ideas or descriptions. Were these difficulties surmountable? If so, how?

2/ What are some problems with using natural language in trying to solve problems? What measures can we take in an attempt to alleviate these problems?

3/ Give an example of a model from your major in school, from one of your hobbies, or from any general field of interest that you have.

4/ What is the purpose of the model you gave in problem 3? Why or why not was this purpose achieved?

5/ Discuss the difficulties involved in making predictions by means of a model. What difficulties are involved in making predictions without a model?

6/ Give an example of a scientific or pseudoscientific model that you are familiar with. Is the subject of this model observable, public, and repeatable? Is this model testable? Give an example of how you might go about testing the model.

7/ Suppose the first three questions on a Gallup poll are:

a/ Are you from the North, South, East, or West?
b/ Are you Democrat, Republican, or other?
c/ Are you younger than 21, 21, or older?

Draw a tree diagram to enumerate the possible replies to these three questions.

8/ Three blindfolded men each choose a hat from a barrel containing three black and two white hats. They stand in a line, with C at the head of the line, B behind C, and A behind B. The men remove their blindfolds and remain facing forward. *A* can see the colors of *B*'s and *C*'s hats, *B* can see only *C*'s hat, and *C* cannot see any hats.

A says, "I don't know what color my hat is."

B says, "I don't know what color my hat is." What color is *C*'s hat? Show this by using a tree diagram.

9/ Earthquakes occur at a particular location at a rate of one a month. The earthquakes can be classified into two categories: those of magnitude *M* or greater, and those of magnitude less than *M*. Use a tree diagram to enumerate all possible sequences of earthquake magnitudes in a four month period.

10/ A person wants to travel from *A* to *B* in Figure 21. Assuming that he can travel only North or East, find the total number of distinct paths that he may take. Note: A path is distinct if there exists no other path that contains exactly the same arcs (that is, line segments connecting two points or nodes.) (Hint: Use a tree diagram.)

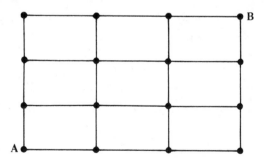

Figure 21. Map for Problem 10.

11/ Use a Venn diagram to investigate the validity of the following arguments:

a/ Premise 1: All *A*'s are *B*'s.
Premise 2: All *B*'s are *C*'s.
Conclusion: All *A*'s are *C*'s.

b/ Premise 1: No *A*'s are *B*'s.
Premise 2: All *B*'s are *C*'s.
Conclusion: No *A*'s are *C*'s.

c/ Premise 1: All A's are B's.
   Premise 2: All C's are B's.
   Conclusion: All A's are C's.

d/ Premise 1: Some A's are B's.
   Premise 2: Some B's are C's.
   Conclusion: Some A's are C's.

e/ Premise 1: If the sun is shining, it is not raining.
   Premise 2: The sun is not shining.
   Conclusion: It is raining.

f/ Premise 1: All engineering professors are eccentric.
   Premise 2: Some geniuses are eccentric.
   Conclusion: All engineering professors are geniuses.

12/ In a college community it is estimated that 70% of the girls have brown eyes. Assume that if a girl has brown eyes, then she does not have blond hair. Find the possible range of the percentage of girls that do not have blond hair. (Hint: Use a Venn diagram.)

3

Uncertainty and the Will to Doubt

playing with uncertainty

It was raining. Sheets of water poured from the skies and whipped around the trees in a surging, howling wind. Peals of thunder rocked the air and lightning illuminated dark grey thunderheads. Professor Gordian was sitting comfortably in front of his fireplace reading the Saturday paper and sipping on his second cup of coffee after breakfast. A knock came at the door, barely audible over the background din of the storm. Professor Gordian lifted himself slowly out of his chair, walked over to the door and opened it. His jaw dropped in amazement at what he saw. Alex was standing at the doorway looking as though he had just climbed fully clothed from a swimming pool.

"Alex, my God! Where have you been?" exclaimed the Professor as he gestured Alex inside.

"Well, this morning started out like one of those rare days that I love. It was overcast and breezy, without being too cold. I decided to walk over to the park and enjoy the morning. After the long walk over there I sat down under a tree for a few minutes to rest, and then it started to rain. The storm came up so quickly that I headed to the closest shelter available—here. But in the 15 minutes that it took me to get here it must have rained an inch!"

"Well, it certainly doesn't look like you were prepared for rain! Here, take this robe and get out of those wet things. I'll put them in the dryer for you."

Alex stripped off his jeans and teeshirt and donned his uncle's robe while Professor Gordian brought some extra towels and put Alex's things in the dryer. Alex was warming himself by the fire when his uncle returned.

"Here's another bad time I can chalk up to the weatherman!" Alex frowned and looked exasperated. "If I only had a dollar for every time I trusted the weatherman's prediction and wasn't prepared for rain, snow, or unbearable heat, I would be rich. On the weather report last night there was a prediction of only a 10 percent chance of rain. But look at it! How can the weather report be so far off? You'd figure that with a 10 percent chance of rain only a few drops would fall, if it rained at all. I haven't seen it rain so hard in my entire life!"

Professor Gordian chuckled at Alex's frustration. "Well, good nephew, I've never seen it rain so hard here either. But you mustn't get so upset with the weatherman. He has a hard job. Next to being a dentist it must be the worst job to have, for a person who wants to feel loved by the public. But really, Alex, you ought to take some responsibility for your bad time yourself, you know. You were warned that there was a 10 percent chance of rain."

"But he said a 10 percent chance, not a 90 percent chance!" Alex protested.

"But Alex, the probability of rain occurring tells you nothing about the severity of rain if it does occur."

Alex looked up quizzically at his uncle. "Huh? What do they mean then by the chance of rain on the weather report?"

"Do you know about probability, Alex?" questioned Professor Gordian.

"I've heard of it, but I'm not exactly sure what it means," admitted Alex.

"The weather man uses probability when he reports the chance **probability** of rain. He has to do this because of the inadequate nature of physical understanding concerning the basic processes that determine the weather. Since no exact prediction can be made, the weatherman has to rely on a statistical prediction. He notes the prevailing conditions of the weather in adjacent areas of the world and notes all of the days in the recorded past that were similar to the day of the prediction. Then he notes what happened on the next day for all of those days in the past. For example, if rain occurred on the succeeding day on 10 percent of all of the similar days in the past, then the weatherman would announce a 10 per-

relative
frequency
definition of
probability
(objective)

cent chance of rain. He is not telling you anything about the severity of the rain if it does occur, only that on like days in the past, 10 percent of the following days had rain. This is one defini-tion of probability. If you take the number of outcomes with a particular attribute and divide it by the total number of outcomes in question, you have the probability of an outcome with that particular attribute. If the weatherman has records for 100 days similar to the day on which he is giving his prediction, and it turned out that on 10 of the following days it rained (rain is the particular attribute), the probability of rain would be 10 out of 100, or 10/100 which is equal to 0.1. The weatherman's way of expressing 0.1 as a percentage, or 10 percent, is more convenient for lay understanding. Nevertheless, probability is usually expressed as a fraction, say 10/100, or as a decimal number, 0.1. This is one definition of probability, but not the only one."

"Hmm. I see, that's interesting. So a 90 percent chance of rain just means that on 90 percent of the days similar to a given day it rained."

"Precisely. Because probability tells you the proportion of times that a given event occurred in the past, you come to expect the event to occur in the future to an extent expressed by its probabil-ity. If it never rained on similar days in the past, the probability of rain would be zero by the definition I just spoke of, and you would not expect it to rain. If on half of the similar days it rained, then the probability would be 0.5, and you would not know whether to expect rain or not. And if on all of the similar days in the past it rained, the probability would be 1.0 and you would expect it to rain.

subjective
definition of
probability

"Another definition of probability is that it is a measure of *degree of belief.* Low probabilities, close to zero, indicate a lack of belief that some condition will occur. High probabilities (close to one) indicate a strong degree of belief, and intermediate probabili-ties indicate an intermediate degree of belief. This is what is known as a *subjective* definition of probability, because it depends on a personal degree of belief. It is a private thing. This is opposed to the other definition of probability in terms of a ratio of outcomes, which is an *objective* definition. Everyone who looked at the data could agree on the ratio of outcomes in question and hence could agree on the probability."

While he was listening to his uncle, a light flashed on in Alex's mind. "Oh! Now I see what Dad meant when he said that he thought that the probability of his favorite candidate becoming president was 0.6. He was just expressing a mild degree of belief that his candidate would win. I was getting confused when you were first talking about probability, because I couldn't understand how his candidate could run for president a number of times and win in 60 percent of the cases."

"Yes, the only reasonable notion of what a probability means when it applies to a single case is in terms of degree of belief. It is possible to assign a probability even when there is only one in-stance of an event, but it will likely be a subjective probability. If I thought the probability that the candidate would win was 0.8, I would be more confident than your father."

Alex thought over what had been said for a moment and then asked, "What about odds? I heard on the radio that there were people in Las Vegas who were predicting odds that a presidential candidate would win or lose. I also hear the same word when peo-ple discuss horse racing."

"Odds are just another way of talking about probability. If the probability of rain is 10/100; that is, if it rained on 10 days out of 100, the odds of rain are 10 to 90. That is to say it rained on 10 days and it did not on 90. In a horse race, odds* like 2 to 1 means that for every three similar encounters that a horse has had, it had won two and lost one. Thus the probability of the horse winning is two out of three or 2/3. Your degree of belief that such a horse will win would be moderately high. Odds, like probability, also ex-presses a degree of belief. Thus, if the odds of a presidential candi-date winning were 5 to 3, it would mean that if you could perform the hypothetical observation of watching the candidate run for president eight times, he would win five times and lose three. The probability of him winning would then be five out of eight or 5/8. But since he is running for president only once, these odds only express a degree of belief that he will win."

odds

---

*The "odds" reported in the news media differ from this concept in that they deal with amounts of money bet on horse races, fights, etc. The use of the term "odds" in the text refers to a more general concept.

Alex leaned back in his seat and looked up at the ceiling. "Now that I think about it, I seem to remember something about probability from when I was younger. I remember someone explaining to me about flipping a coin and how you don't know whether heads or tails will come up. But I remember something about the probability of a head being 1/2 not because of a degree of belief, but because there are two sides to a coin and only one head. That doesn't seem to apply to either of the definitions you have told me about. I can see that the probability of tossing a head on a coin might be 1/2 because I have absolutely no idea whether the outcome on a single toss would be heads or tails, and I can also see why it might be 1/2 if you flipped a coin, say 1,000 times, and you got 500 heads. But how does one head in two sides fit in?"

objective probability as ratio of number of equally likely outcomes

"You are speaking of still another definition of probability. This is another objective definition which deals with the probability of what is called an event. An event is an aggregation of one or more outcomes. For example, you can speak of the event of flipping a head on a coin, or the event of flipping two coins and getting two heads, or the event of rolling a die and getting an even number. According to the definition you referred to, the probability of an event is equal to the number of outcomes in which the event occurs divided by the total number of possible outcomes, provided that all outcomes are equally likely. For example, when flipping a coin two equally likely outcomes are possible, a head or a tail. Since only one of these outcomes is a head, the probability of a head is one out of two, or 1/2, or 0.5. Another example would be rolling an even number on a die. There are three outcomes which result in an even number, namely, rolling a 2, a 4, or a 6. Six equally likely outcomes are possible, rolling a 1, a 2, a 3, a 4, a 5, or a 6. So the probability of getting an even number is three out of six or 3/6, or 0.5. Notice that all of the definitions of probability that we have mentioned are related in some way. For example, with a coin, since there is no reason to favor one of the outcomes of heads or tails more than the other, you would expect to find that if you tossed the coin a large number of times you would get about half heads and half tails. You might toss a coin ten times and get seven heads and three tails for a ratio of 0.7. If you tossed it 100 times, you might get 58 heads for a ratio of 0.58. And if you tossed it 1,000 times, you might get 520 heads for a ratio of 0.52. These ratios correspond to one notion of probability. It is the same ratio notion that the weatherman uses. Notice that the more times you toss the coin the closer the ratio of heads to total tosses is to 0.5. This is an interesting result and it is one thing that allows us to state that the two sides of the coin are equally likely in the first place. Generally, our subjective notions of probability, that is to say our degrees of belief, are often learned from the objective observations that we make. We have found that about half of the times that we flip a fair coin we get a head, and there is no reason to suspect that one side is any more likely to occur than the other. We therefore assign a subjective degree of belief to getting a head on the single toss of a coin as 0.5.

"This reminds me of an interesting experiment that you can perform when you get bored." Professor Gordian reached over to his desk and opened a drawer and pulled out a thumb tack. "If I flip this thumb tack as I would a coin and note whether it comes to rest on the floor with the point up, or obliquely on both its head and point, what probability would you assign to the event of landing with the point up?"

Alex carefully examined the thumbtack and stated flatly, "I think that the probability of it landing with the point up is 80 percent. I think that it probably would balance better with the head down, and I always seem to be getting the things stuck in the soles of my shoes at school. That is something that wouldn't happen if most of the thumbtacks landed point down."

Professor Gordian smiled. "Most of us have a lot of experience flipping coins but very little experience flipping thumbtacks. I think that if you try the experiment of flipping this tack a large number of times, you will find that your assessment of the probability is pretty far off from the ratio of point up occurrences to total number of flips."

Alex grinned. "You're really going to make me flip this thing a hundred times to find out the answer?"

"I hate to deprive you of a valuable life experience by telling you, Alex. And besides, you might not even believe me if I told you. You would probably end up doing the experiment anyway, so I'll just keep you in suspense."

"Oh well. I'll wait to do this until later, because my fingers are still numb from the cold. But tell me—I'm still curious about the weatherman. It seems that there should be some better method of forecasting the weather—one that takes into account the severity of a storm as well as the probability of one occurring. Knowing the probability alone does not allow you to make very good preparations for a walk or a picnic!"

"I have often thought the same thing myself, Alex. And I think

71

I have come up with a better method for reporting the weather forecast. It incorporates not only the probability of a storm, but also its intensity. It is based on another notion of probability known as *expected value.* An expected value is the average amount of payoff that occurs in an uncertain situation over many repetitions."

"Aha! So it is what you might expect to receive on any given average occasion?"

"Yes, that is true. But since it is just an average you might not ever receive exactly that amount of payoff. However, the average is in some sense representative of all of the values of which it is an average. Let me show you more specifically what I mean by expected value, and then I will give you an example of what I am talking about."

Professor Gordian reached over to his desk and pulled out a pad and a sheet of paper. He started to sketch some notes for Alex as he talked.

"Let's suppose that the weatherman has records for 100 days similar to today, and he wants to make a prediction for tomorrow. He notes that on ten of the days in the records it rained an inch on each succeeding day. For the remaining 90 following days it did not rain. Expected value gives you the amount of rainfall for each day averaged over the 100-day period. You can compute this fairly readily by the following method. First you calculate the total amount of rainfall in the 100-day period. Since it rained one inch on each of ten days, you multiply one by ten and get ten inches. It rained zero inches on 90 days, so multiplication gives you zero inches total for these days. Ten plus zero gives a total of ten inches of rain for the 100 days. Now you can divide this total amount of rain by the total number of days to give you the average per day. Ten divided by 100 equals 1/10 inch per day.

"In general, there is a simple method to calculate expected value. If I rearrange the work I just did, you can see what I am talking about."

Professor Gordian wrote down the following:

$$\text{total rain} = 10(1) + 90(0)$$
$$= 10 \text{ inches of rain}$$

$$\text{expected value} = \frac{\text{total amount of rain}}{\text{total number of days}} = \frac{10(1) + 90(0)}{100}$$

$$= \frac{10(1)}{100} + \frac{90(0)}{100} = \frac{10}{100}(1) + \frac{90}{100}(0)$$

= (probability of rain) × (amount of rain on rainy day) + (probability of no rain) × (amount of rain on nonrainy day)

"In this example I have been talking about the amount of rain on days that it did not rain. Normally I would just ignore this quantity since it is zero, but I want to write it down here so I can develop a general formula for all cases. Notice that if I distribute the total number of days in the denominator to each term of the sum I get the probability of each event times the payoff associated with each event, all summed together for all events.

"You can calculate expected value for any situation by this general formula," said Professor Gordian as he wrote down the equation:

$$EV = \Sigma P(E)V(E)$$

formula for expected value

"In this formula the symbol $P(E)$ stands for the probability of an event, and $V(E)$ stands for the amount of payoff associated with that event. The symbol Σ directs you to add up all of the products $P(E)$ × $V(E)$ obtained from each event."

"Hey, that's neat!" exclaimed Alex. "Now I can see what you meant about the expected value giving you some value that you might never get exactly on any given occasion. On those days recorded, it never did rain 1/10 of an inch on any single day. It either rained one inch or not at all. But at least expected value gives you some idea of the total amount of rain distributed over the total number of days in question. If I knew that the expected value of rain was 1/10 of an inch I would take an umbrella with me, whereas I might not if I were just informed that the probability of rain were 0.1."

Professor Gordian got up and started for the kitchen. "Would you like some coffee, Alex?"

"Yes, please. Say, this concept of expected value seems like it should have other applications as well. It just occurred to me that you might be able to use the concept of expected value to determine how good or bad a deal you were getting on a bet or gamble."

"Yes, that is an excellent application of expected value. You consider a bet or gamble to be fair if over the long run the net gain

"fair" games

or loss of each participant is zero. This is so when the expected value is zero."

Alex smiled. "I suppose that none of the games in Las Vegas are fair in that sense, because the casino operators must be making money."

"That's true. All of the games in Las Vegas, save perhaps one, give the advantage to the house. You can even use the concept of expected value to choose the 'best' games; that is, the ones with the least expected value of loss for you. Would you like to try to figure out the expected value for some game?"

"Sure! Let me see . . . how about roulette. Roulette has always had some strange sort of fascination for me."

"OK, Alex, but roulette is very complicated, so why don't you take a special case. First start with the simplest type of bet—betting on color. As you know, there are 38 numbers on the roulette wheel. Eighteen of them are red, 18 are black, and two are green. You can place your money on a color, say red, and if that color comes up in the next turn you get back the amount of money that you bet, along with the same amount extra as a prize for winning. If any other color comes up, you lose whatever you bet. These rules apply only for betting on either red or black. Betting on green is a different story. Why don't you find the expected value for betting on red?"

"Okay!" said Alex as he enthusiastically reached over to get the paper and pencil from his uncle. "There are two events of interest here. Either I win or I lose. If I bet on red, the outcomes in which I win are the 18 numbers which are red, and the total outcomes are the 38 numbers of any color. Therefore the probability of winning is 18/38. The ways in which I can lose are the 20 numbers which are not red. So the probability of losing is 20/38. All I need now are the values associated with winning and losing. Let's say that I bet $1. If I win, I gain $1 and if I lose, I lose $1. Hmmm."

Alex stared at the figures he had written on the sheet of paper.

"What's wrong?" asked his uncle.

"I'm not sure what to do with the values for winning and losing. We only looked at positive values before, such as the amount of rain that would fall."

"Try thinking about it this way, Alex. Anything you win you add to what you already have, and anything you lose you subtract from what you have. If the net expected value is positive it means that you will receive money, and if it is negative, it means that you will have to pay."

"Oh, I see. If I use positive numbers for winnings and negative numbers for losses, then that will be reflected in the expected value. Let me plug into the formula."

Alex wrote the following on the sheet of paper:

$$EV = \Sigma P(E)\; V(E)$$

$$= \underbrace{18/38}_{\substack{\text{probability} \\ \text{of winning}}} \underbrace{(\$1)}_{\substack{\text{value of} \\ \text{winning}}} + \underbrace{20/38}_{\substack{\text{probability} \\ \text{of losing}}} \underbrace{(-\$1)}_{\substack{\text{value of} \\ \text{losing}}}$$

$$= 2/38\;(-\$1), \text{ or about } -\$0.05$$

The expected value is a loss of about $0.05 if I always bet $1 on red. Say, this is not a very good game to play! Every time I play I will lose a nickel!"

"It's a good game to play if you enjoy it! And remember, if you bet $1 on each game, you will never lose exactly $.05 on any given game. That is just the average that you would expect to lose over a large number of games. On any single game you will either win $1 or lose $1. And if you are lucky, you can win the majority of games that you play and walk off with a large profit. This is not too likely, but nevertheless it is possible."

"And it is the kind of thing you hope for when you go to Las Vegas," said Alex with a grin. "That was interesting. I want to try to figure out the expected values for other games. How about dice games?"

"Why don't you try it for craps? To keep it simple, just suppose that you are rolling a pair of dice and you are betting to win on the first roll. Say you will win if you roll a seven and will lose otherwise. Go ahead and give it a try."

Alex attacked the problem with enthusiasm. "The first thing I will need to do is to calculate the respective probabilities of winning and losing. Let's see, the number of ways of rolling a seven is. . . " Alex rolled his eyes to the left. "This is not easy. Let me make a tree."

Alex sketched out the tree shown in Figure 22 to enumerate all the possible outcomes in the roll of two dice.

He then started counting up the total number of outcomes and the number of outcomes in which seven occurred. "There are six outcomes in which the numbers on the dice total seven, and there are thirty six possible outcomes, so the probability of rolling a

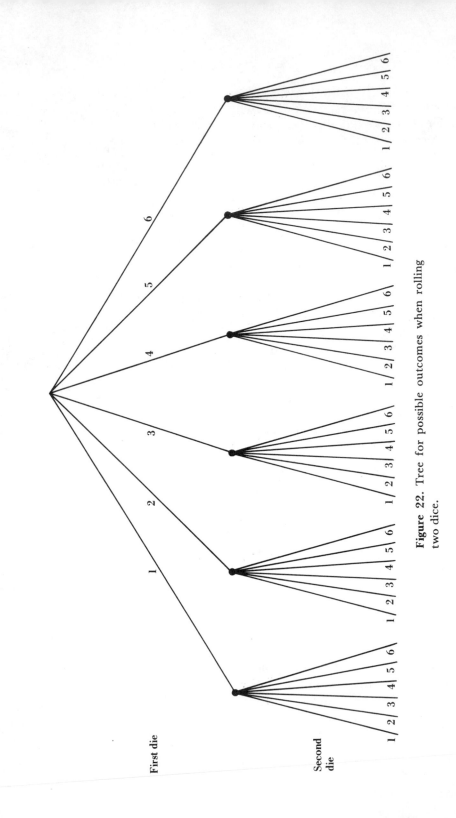

Figure 22. Tree for possible outcomes when rolling two dice.

seven is 6/36. Isn't there some fancy way to figure this out without enumerating all of the possibilities in a tree and counting them?"

"There is a 'fancier' way, but it wouldn't make this particular problem any easier. The other way is especially useful when you are working on problems where a complete tree might be cumbersome or very time consuming to construct, or when you are dealing with subjective probabilities, where the representation of a probability as the number of outcomes with a particular attribute divided by the total number of outcomes is not very meaningful. The 'fancier' way involves two general rules for manipulating probabilities directly."

Alex lit up with curiosity. "Could you show me?"

Professor Gordian beamed. "Sure! I wish all of my students had the same enthusiasm as you. That's what makes teaching so enjoyable." Professor Gordian took back the pencil and paper from Alex and started to explain. He pointed to Alex's tree diagram for the craps game. "Notice what you have done here. The outcomes for each of the two dice are *independent,* that is to say the out- come on one die does not affect the outcome on the other. You recognized this fact when you drew your tree. Notice that for each outcome on the first die, you have shown that all of the possible outcomes on the second die could occur. For any given outcome on the first die, there are six possible outcomes on the second die. You could compute the total number of possibilities when you toss both dice together by multiplying six, which is the number of outcomes on the first die, by six, which is the number of outcomes possible on the second die regardless of the outcome on the first. This multiplication will give you the total number of branches in your tree. There are 36 possibilities. You can count the number of outcomes with a certain attribute in the same manner. For example, suppose you wanted to compute the probability of an even number appearing on each of the dice. You could make a separate tree for this, like so." Professor Gordian drew the tree shown in Figure 23.

He pointed out to Alex, "You can see that there are three ways to get an even number on the first die, and there are three ways to get an even number on the second die regardless of what occurs on the first. You could multiply three times three and get nine, which is the total number of ways to get an even number on each die. The probability of rolling an even number on each die would then be 9/36 = 1/4.

"It is possible to use this principle to calculate the probabilities of given outcomes occurring together. The principle involved is

independent outcomes

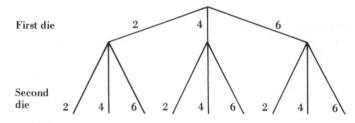

Figure 23. Tree for rolling two dice and getting only even numbers.

multiplicative
rule

embodied in the *multiplicative rule* which states that the probability of two events occurring together is the product of the probability of one event and the probability of the other event given the condition that the first event has occurred."

Professor Gordian wrote the following formula:

$$P(A \cap B) = P(A)P(B|A)$$

"The formula that I have written is read 'the probability of events A and B occurring together is equal to the probability of

conditional
probability

A times the probability of B given A. This last probability, that of B given A, is called a *conditional probability*. It is the probability of B under the condition that A has already occurred."

Alex looked at the paper with a perplexed expression on his face. His uncle hurried to clarify his explanation by pulling a deck of cards out of his desk drawer and shuffling them.

"Perhaps an example or two will clarify what I mean by the concept of a conditional probability. Here I have a regular bridge deck of fifty two cards. If I ask you to pick a card at random from the deck, what is the probability that it is a red card?"

"It is 1/2 since half of the cards are red," answered Alex.

"Fine. Now suppose that you pick a card and it is red, and then I ask you to put that card on the table and pick another card from what is left in the deck. What is the probability that you will pick another red card?"

"Well, there would be 51 cards left and 25 of them would be red. It would be 25/51."

dependent
events

"Right. This second probability of 25/51 is the conditional probability of picking a red card, given the condition that you have already picked a red card from the deck. Notice that the two probabilities that you have just computed are not the same. That is because the two events are not independent. They are dependent—

78

the probability of picking a second red card from the deck is altered by picking the first red card. If you had taken the first red card and replaced it in the deck and I had reshuffled before you had drawn the second card, what would be the probability of a second red card then?"

"One half again, because the deck would be the same as the first time that I picked a card. The two events of picking a red card would then be independent, because the drawing of the first red card would not influence the probability of the second red card. Am I correct?"

"Yes, you are correct. There is nothing really mysterious about the notion of a conditional probability. In fact, *all* probabilities are conditional, only most of the conditions are usually not specified, or are assumed to be understood. When I ask you to tell me what the probability of a red card is, it is understood that the deck has 52 cards and half of them are red and the deck is shuffled and you are picking randomly, and so on and so on. These conditions are understood, so there is no reason to write them. But with something like picking a second red card when the first card is not replaced, it is important to specify the new conditions.

"Now that you understand what a conditional probability is, let me go back to the formula for events A and B occurring together. Let me use it to calculate the probability of rolling even numbers on each of two dice. The formula says that you can get the probability of rolling even numbers on both die A and die B by multiplying the probability of rolling an even number on die A by the probability of rolling an even number on die B given that you have already rolled an even number on die A. To begin, what is the probability of rolling an even number on die A?"

"Well, it is 1/2, and so is the probability of B given A, because the outcome of the first die has nothing to do with the outcome of the second die. The two events are independent, right?"

"Quite right. When you now multiply 1/2 by 1/2 you get 1/4, which is the probability of rolling an even number on each die. Pretty neat, eh?"

"Yeah! But why does it work?"

"I was just getting to that. Notice what you have done when you multiplied the probabilities together. To multiply two fractions together, you multiply the numerators together and place that product over the product of the denominators. When you look at what you have in the numerator of each expression, you see that you have the number of ways in which die A can be even and the number of ways in which die B can be even, respectively.

Multiplying these two numbers together is like calculating the number of ways in which die A and die B can both be even at the same time. You could calculate this by constructing a tree as we have already done. The number of branches at the bottom would be the product of the number of ways that die A could be even and the number of ways that die B could be even." Professor Gordian referred back to the tree (Figure 24) that he had drawn before. "See?"

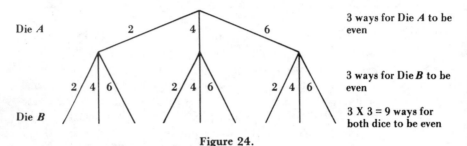

Figure 24.

"Yes, I see. And the same thing holds true for the denominators. You can find the total number of outcomes for the two dice together by multiplying the total number of outcomes for die A by the total number of outcomes for die B. And this is exactly what you do when you multiply probabilities. You end up with the total number of outcomes in the denominator, and the number of outcomes in which both attributes occur together in the numerator. That's very clever!"

Professor Gordian nodded. "It saves a lot of time in certain instances when we can apply this rule. You can now answer the question of what is the probability of some combination of outcomes when rolling two dice. Suppose I asked you what is the probability of rolling the two dice and getting a one on each?"

"The probability of getting a one on a single die is 1/6, and the probability of getting a one on the other die given that there is a one on the first die is also 1/6, because the two events are independent. The probability of a one on both dice is therefore 1/6 times 1/6 or 1/36."

"Good. You can use this rule along with a tree to develop a very powerful problem solving tool. Look at this."

Professor Gordian took the original tree that Alex had drawn to enumerate all of the possible outcomes of rolling two dice. He then wrote in the probabilities associated with each outcome as shown in Figure 25.

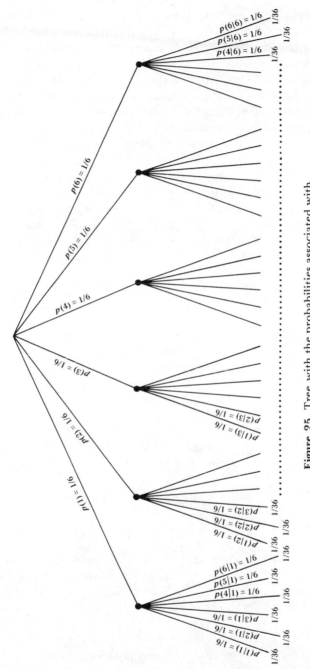

Figure 25. Tree with the probabilities associated with rolling two dice.

"We can label each branch for die A with its associated probability of 1/6. In the lower level of the tree we can identify each branch with its associated conditional probability, $P(B|A)$. For example, P(3/4) is the probability of a 3 on die B given a 4 showed on die A. It is a conditional probability because each branch in the lower level assumes the occurrence of some particular outcome of die A. If you want to calculate the probability of any of the joint outcomes identified at the bottom of the tree, that is, any combination of the outcomes of die A and die B, then all you have to do is multiply the probabilities on the branches leading to that endpoint. For example, to obtain the probability of rolling a six on each die, multiply the probability of a six on the first die, P(6) = 1/6, times the probability of a six on the second die given a six on the first die, P(6/6) = 1/6, to get 1/36. You can formulate a general rule for this manipulation—multiply down a tree to get the probabilities associated with the outcome or event identified by the terminal points.

multiplying
down a tree

"There is still another rule for manipulating probabilities. This rule is called the additive rule and deals with situations where you have *mutually exclusive* events. Mutually exclusive events are events that cannot occur together. An example would be picking a single card that is red and black at the same time. You can pick either a red card or a black card from a deck, but you cannot have both colors at the same time because there is no single card that is both red and black. Another example would be rolling a one and a two at the same time on a die—it cannot be done. Obtaining one outcome precludes the other. The additive rule states that when you have mutually exclusive events you can find the probability of one or another of them occurring by adding the respective probabilities.

mutually
exclusive
events

additive rule

Professor Gordian wrote the following formula on the pad:

$$P(A \cup B) = P(A) + P(B) \quad \text{if } A \text{ and } B \text{ are mutually exclusive}$$

"The symbol $\cup$ is, read 'OR', and so $A \cup B$ stands for 'A or B.' This includes the case where A and B both occur together, designated earlier by $A \cap B$. $A \cup B$ could really be read 'A or B or both.' An example of the use of this formula would be in calculating the probability of rolling a one or a two on a die in a single roll. The events are mutually exclusive because they cannot occur at the same time on a single die. The probability of rolling a one is 1/6 and the probability of rolling a two is 1/6, so the probability of rolling a one or a two is 1/6 + 1/6 or 2/6. The reason why this works is that when adding fractions you add the numerators, but the denominator remains the same. Thus, when you add probabilities you are adding up the numerators. This will give you the total number of outcomes with either attribute. In the roll of a die there is one way in which a one can occur, and there is one way in which a two can occur. The total number of outcomes, six, does not change, and so the denominator remains the same. But you can add the numerators to get the number of ways in which a one or a two can occur. This explanation applies only when the two probabilities have the same denominator. If the denominators are different, for example, when you want to calculate the probability of rolling a one on a die and picking a red card from a bridge deck, the explanation becomes somewhat more involved. The same principle holds, but I will leave the explanation for you to figure out later.

"A more complex example of the use of this rule is in computing the probability of getting a total of seven when rolling a pair of dice. Look at the tree you drew with all of the probabilities drawn in for the throw of two dice. You can see at the bottom of the tree that there are six mutually exclusive ways to roll a seven. You can get a one on the first die and a six on the second, a two on the first and a five on the second, a three and a four, a four and a three, a five and a two, or finally, a six and a one. The probability of each of these combinations is 1/36. Therefore, by the additive rule, the probability of any one or another of them occurring is 1/36 + 1/36 + 1/36 + 1/36 + 1/36 + 1/36 which is equal to 6/36.

"There is a general principle in all of this. Whenever you have a tree diagram such as the ones we have been examining, the terminal points at the bottom of the tree will represent mutually exclusive events. To obtain the probability of any one or another of them occurring, all you have to do is to add together the respective probabilities across the bottom of the tree. The second rule is: add across a tree. *adding across a tree*

"While I'm at it, I should probably add one final thought about tree diagrams and probabilities. Normally you will have trees in which the branches below each node represent mutually exclusive *exhaustive possibilities* and *exhaustive* possibilities. The meaning of exhaustive is that all of the possibilities are represented—there is no other possibility that is not listed. When this is the case, the sum of the probabilities of the branches immediately below such a node must equal one. This is true because one or another of these possibilities *must* occur. The probability for one or another of them occurring is therefore one. This consideration will sometimes allow you to very quickly compute the probabilities which are not given to you. For example, if you know that the probability of rain tomorrow is 0.1, then you can immediately figure out that the probability of no rain tomorrow must be 0.9, because 1.0 - 0.1 = 0.9. It must either rain or not rain tomorrow—they are two mutually exclusive, exhaustive possibilities."

"Hey, this stuff is super! I like it just because it is fun to play with. But tell me—you mentioned a while ago about there being some types of problems that are not amenable to a solution by a tree alone because they involve subjective probabilities. I think that is how we first got onto the subject of using algebraic principles of probability manipulation. Can you give me an example of what you were talking about?"

"I sure can, Alex. Your friend Greg was just by my office the other day to talk to me concerning his future. It seems that he either wants to become a doctor or a dentist—he's not quite sure which yet. He had gotten advice from several people. Talking to his counselor at school, he found out that if he applied to medical school he had about a 50-50 chance of getting in. His counselor also told him that if he applied to dental school, his chances were much better, about 3 to 1 odds. He also found out that about 9/10 of all the students entering medical school finally make it through to get a degree, and also about 9/10 of all entering dental students make it through to finally become dentists. His question to me was, given all of this information that he had collected, what were the chances of him actually becoming either a doctor or a dentist?

"The first step in helping him was to make a tree for all of the possibilities facing him. I tried to make the tree so that the branches under each node represented mutually exclusive, exhaustive possibilities. This was made easier by Greg's assurance that he would definitely either apply to medical school or to dental school, but not to both. I drew out this tree for him." Professor Gordian sketched out the tree in Figure 26 for Alex.

"After I drew this tree for Greg, the next step was to put in the relevant probabilities. I started out by asking him whether he thought it was more likely that he would apply to medical or dental school. He answered that he had no idea which of the two he would eventually do, but he would definitely do one or the other. Since his knowledge of which he would do was no different from

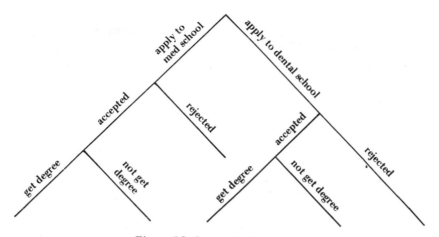

Figure 26. Greg's decision tree.

his knowledge of the outcome of the flip of a coin, we assigned a probability of 1/2 to each of these possibilities.

"The next step was to fill in the probabilities in the second level of the tree. On the left, we have the probability of being accepted given that he has applied to med school, and the probability of being rejected given that he has applied to med school. His counselor told him that the probability of being accepted was 1/2, so we filled that in. Since we know that being accepted and being rejected are mutually exclusive and exhaustive, we know that their probabilities must add to 1. That means that the probability of being rejected given that he applies to med school must also be 1/2. On the right side of the tree, we had to consider the probabilities of being accepted and being rejected given that Greg applies to dental school. From what his counselor told him, we filled in the probability of being accepted as 3/4. Since the probability of being accepted and being rejected must sum to 1, we know that the probability of being rejected given that he applies to dental school must be 1/4.

"Going down to the third level of the tree, on the left we had to consider the probability of his getting a degree given that he is accepted to med school, and the probability of him not getting his degree given that he is accepted. From statistical records, Greg deduced that the probability of him getting his degree given that he was accepted is 9/10. Since the probability of getting the degree and not getting the degree must sum to 1, he knows that the probability of not getting his degree must be 1/10. On the right of the tree, we were concerned about the probability of him getting a dental degree given that he is accepted to dental school. Also from statistics, Greg deduced that the probability of him getting a dental degree given that he was accepted was 9/10. The probability of him not getting the degree must then be 1/10 because the probabilities of the two branches must sum to 1. Getting the degree and not getting the degree are mutually exclusive and exhaustive.

"Looking at this tree Greg was interested in only two outcomes, that of getting a medical degree and that of getting a dental degree. He could find the probability of one or the other occurring by simply adding the probabilities of the individual events. This is an application of the additive rule—you can add across a tree diagram. But in order to do this he must first compute what the individual probabilities are for getting a medical degree and getting a dental degree. To get a medical degree he must apply to medical school, be accepted, and then get his degree. So the probability he was concerned with was the probability of applying to med school *and* being accepted *and* getting his degree. This probability can be calculated by multiplying the probability of applying to medical school by the probability of getting the degree given that he is accepted. This is an application of the multiplicative rule—you can multiply down a tree diagram. This probability would then be 1/2 × 1/2 × 9/10, which equals 9/40. To get a dental degree, he must apply to dental school, be accepted, and get his dental degree. Therefore, the probability he was interested in was that of applying to dental school *and* being accepted *and* getting his degree. This can be calculated just like the probabilities for medical school—by multiplying down the tree diagram. This gives us 1/2 × 3/4 × 9/10, which is 27/80. Now we compute the probability of getting a medical degree or a dental degree. This is 9/40 + 27/80 which is equal to 45/80, or about 0.56. Thus, it is moderately likely that he will get a medical or dental degree. In fact, it is more likely than not that he will get a degree. Knowing Greg, I am sure that he will plan his future accordingly."

The final tree that Professor Gordian developed for Greg's situation is shown in Figure 27. When Professor Gordian had finished, Alex examined the tree that his uncle had drawn on the pad. "This is an amazing technique for integrating all of the given sources of information. Not only have you condensed a lot of diverse sources of information, but you have combined objective and subjective sources. I'm impressed!"

Professor Gordian looked pleased. "I find this technique very

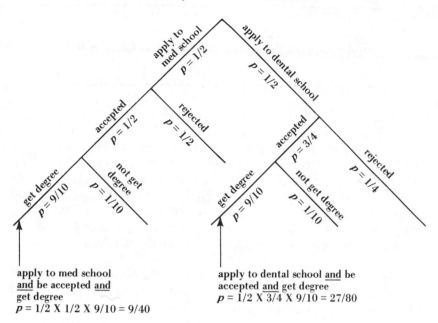

apply to med school
and be accepted and
get degree
$p = 1/2 \times 1/2 \times 9/10 = 9/40$

apply to dental school and be
accepted and get degree
$p = 1/2 \times 3/4 \times 9/10 = 27/80$

get med degree or get dental degree = 9/40 + 27/80 = 0.56

Figure 27. Greg's decision tree with probabilities added.

useful, too. I use it at least once a week for some application or another. People often make decisions based on inadequate or fragmentary knowledge, and this is often due to an inability to incorporate many diverse sources of information into their analysis at the same time. The model I have just shown you allows you to take into account more information than a person normally does, and thus helps you get the whole picture."

Professor Gordian paused, looked out the window and announced with a cheery voice, "Hey! It's stopped raining!"

Alex also looked out the window and then at his watch. "And it's a good thing, too. I had better be getting home. I have a lot of studying to do for next week. Say! We never did figure out the expected value for the dice game."

"I'm afraid we got sidetracked, Alex. But I hope you learned something valuable today. Even if it was only to carry an umbrella."

"I have learned a lot more than that, Professor. I learned not to come over here and expect to get any answers. Now I have to hurry home so I can flip a thumbtack!"

87

should you see another doctor?

It was late in the evening when Alex left the research library. He had managed to find some statistical data on the rare disease that afflicted his close friend Joe. He had summarized the information in a table which he was squinting to see as he was walking in the moonlight. The data is shown in Figure 28. Of a sample of 1,000 people who had had the disease only 200 had survived. Of the 200 that had survived, 120 had been operated upon and 80 had survived with no operation. What was Joe to do? Undergo the operation or not?

Alex inspected the various conditions. Suppose Joe decides on the operation. If the past records could serve as an indication of what is likely to happen to him, we have:

$$P\text{ (Survive|Operation)} \quad = \frac{120}{360}$$

$$P\text{ (Not survive|Operation)} \quad = \frac{240}{360}$$

With no operation:

$$P\text{ (Survive|No operation)} \quad = \frac{80}{640}$$

$$P\text{ (Not survive|No operation)} = \frac{560}{640}$$

In each case the probability of survival is a ratio of two numbers. The number in the denominator represents the number of people in the stipulated condition. For example, if we focus on the people who were operated upon then the denominator is 360, and for those who were not operated upon the number is 640. The numerator represents the number of people with a particular attribute among the total number within the condition. For example, within the condition of "operated," one attribute may be "survived"—

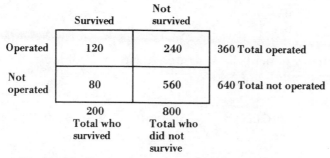

	Survived	Not survived	
Operated	120	240	360 Total operated
Not operated	80	560	640 Total not operated
	200 Total who survived	800 Total who did not survive	

Figure 28. Treatment and survival record for 1000 persons with a disease.

represented by the number 120, and the other attribute may be "not survived"—represented by the number 240.

Using the numbers in Figure 28 we can write the following probability statements:

(S stands for *Survive*, and $\bar{S}$ for *Not survive*)
(OP stands for *Operate,* and $\overline{OP}$ for *Not operate*)

Given that a patient was operated upon (first row), the total in the given condition is 360:

$$P(S|OP) = \frac{120}{360}, \text{ or 1 out of 3, or 1/3}$$

$$P(\bar{S}|OP) = \frac{240}{360}, \text{ or 2 out of 3, or 2/3}$$

Given that a patient was not operated upon (second row), the total in the given condition is 640:

$$P(S|\overline{OP}) = \frac{80}{640}, \text{ or 1 out of 8, or 1/8}$$

$$P(\bar{S}|\overline{OP}) = \frac{560}{640}, \text{ or 7 out of 8, or 7/8}$$

Given that a patient survived (first column), the total in the given condition is 200:

$$P(OP|S) = \frac{120}{200}, \text{ or 6 out of 10, or 6/10}$$

$$P(\overline{OP}|S) = \frac{80}{200}, \text{ or 4 out of 10, or } 4/10$$

Given that a patient did not survive (second column), the total in the given condition is 800:

$$P(OP|\overline{S}) = \frac{240}{800}, \text{ or 3 out of 10, or } 3/10$$

$$P(\overline{OP}|\overline{S}) = \frac{560}{800}, \text{ or 7 out of 10, or } 7/10$$

The classification of the numbers in each box of Figure 28 is obtained by reading the label of the row of the box *"Operated"* or *"Not operated"* and the label of the column of the box *"Survived"* or *"Not survived."*

This can be summarized by using labels as shown in Figure 29 (the numbers indicate the number of people in each category).

The same classification can be shown using a tree diagram, as shown in Figure 30. Beginning with columns S and $\overline{S}$ we record the total number for S and $\overline{S}$, that is, the 200 people who survived out of the original 1,000, and the 800 who did not survive out of the original 1,000. Going down the left branch S, we take 120 out of 200 (or 120/200) for $OP|S$, so that 120 people have the classification $S \cap OP$. 80/200 are $\overline{OP}|S$, yielding 80 with classification $S \cap \overline{OP}$. The classification labels and numbers at the ends of the remaining two branches from $\overline{S}$ are generated in similar fashion.

A tree can also be constructed by beginning the branches of the tree with the row classifications OP and $\overline{OP}$ and then continuing with the column classifications, as shown in Figure 31.

There are only four basic numbers given in the original table,

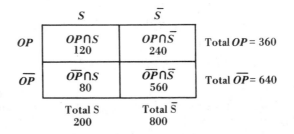

	S	$\overline{S}$	
OP	$OP \cap S$ 120	$OP \cap \overline{S}$ 240	Total OP = 360
$\overline{OP}$	$\overline{OP} \cap S$ 80	$\overline{OP} \cap \overline{S}$ 560	Total $\overline{OP}$ = 640
	Total S 200	Total $\overline{S}$ 800	

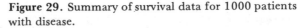

Figure 29. Summary of survival data for 1000 patients with disease.

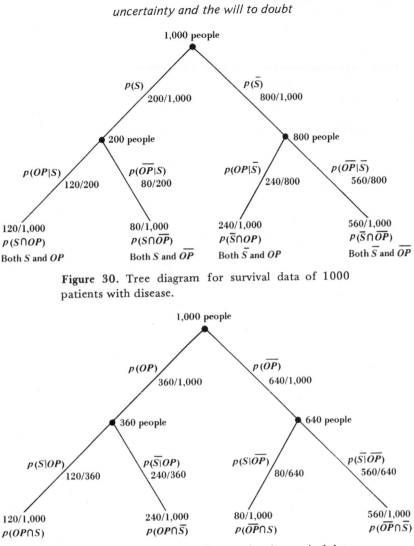

Figure 30. Tree diagram for survival data of 1000 patients with disease.

Figure 31. Another tree diagram for the survival data of 1000 patients with disease.

yet there are so many different ways of looking at them. But the basic question remains—*what to do*? If we accept the data of the past as a reasonable guide to predict the future, which is better, to operate, or not to operate? Two hundred out of the total of 1,000 survived, i.e., one out of five. But of the 360 who were operated upon, 120, or one out of three, survived. Of the 640 who were not operated upon, 80, or one out of eight, survived. The odds are better for an operation.

Alex thought it was important to have tools to structure the problem so that one can represent the uncertainties involved in the different courses of action (OP, $\overline{OP}$) and associated states (S, $\overline{S}$). But suddenly he stopped and sensed excitement mounting within himself as he remembered the problem solving guide Professor Gordian had acquainted him with: "Have a will to doubt." It occurred to him that he had not questioned the premise that Joe was sick in the first place. After all, the diagnosis of the disease was based on a test, and there are uncertainties associated with test results. Alex recalled the time when he served as the subject of a medical test in the army. He was one of 1,000 soldiers who volunteered to participate in an experiment. Four hundred of them were given a mild form of a disease, and then all 1,000 were subjected to a test that was supposed to detect the presence or absence of the disease. The test indicated either positive results P, signaling presence of the disease, or negative results $\overline{P}$, signaling absence of the disease.

The results of the experiment were as shown in Figure 32. D stands for people who had the disease and $\overline{D}$ for those who did not. If the test were perfect then the experiment would have resulted in the table of Figure 33. However, the actual results showed that the test was sometimes wrong. Forty cases of people with the disease got negative test results, and 120 cases of people without the disease got positive test results.

"'Have a will to doubt'—what an important guide to problem solving," Alex reflected, as he rushed into the house eager to study the implications of this guide to Joe's illness.

Alex had no data on the test that Joe had taken, but he decided

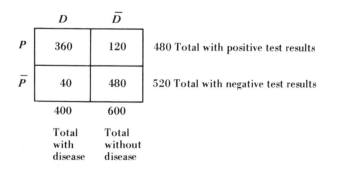

Figure 32. Results of a test of soldiers with and without disease.

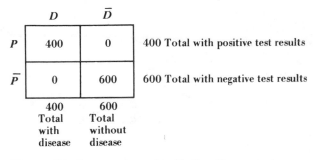

Figure 33. Expected results if the disease test was perfect.

to apply the table that represented his own army experience to Joe's case. If these same numbers were used in Joe's case, then Joe would be classified as one of the 480 people out of 1,000 who had positive test results. Of these, only 360 actually had the disease, while 120 did not. There is, therefore, a probability of 120 in 480, or one out of four that he is O.K.

"Now I have a new problem," thought Alex. "I'm not certain that Joe has the disease in the first place. How can I dispel some of the uncertainty?"

It's often strange how the mind works, but now, of all times, Alex remembered a joke that had been told in the army. It was about three soldiers who had been subjected to deadly radiation and were told by the examining doctor that they had three days to live. When each was asked for his wishes, two gave elaborate descriptions for exotic events from the first day's breakfast to the last day's supper. The third one said quietly, "I want to see another doctor."

That's it—Joe should see another doctor and take another test to help dispel the uncertainty.

In fact, if the test presented in Figure 32 were to be administered again to the same 1,000 people, the results would be as shown in Figure 34.

P_1 and P_2 indicate positive test results in the first and second examination, respectively. The symbol ∩ for *and* has been left out, so that $p(DP_1P_2)$, for example, stands for the probability of a person have disease D and getting positive results in two tests, P_1 and P_2. This would have been denoted $P(D \cap P_1 \cap P_2)$ before.

We assume the second test will have the same record of accuracy of disease detection as the first test (shown in Figure 32). That is, if a person has the disease (the four left branches of the tree), then

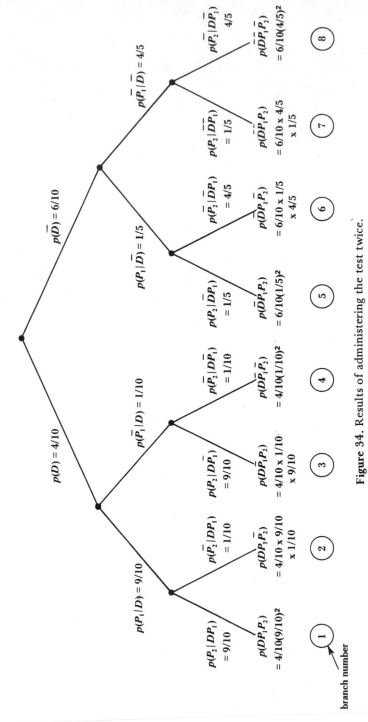

Figure 34. Results of administering the test twice.

in 360 out of 400, or in 9/10 of the cases, the test will be positive, and in 40 out of 400, or in 1/10 of the cases, the test will be negative. Similarly, if a person does not have the disease (the four right branches of the tree), then in 120 out of 600, or in 1/5 of the cases, the test will be positive, and in 480 out of 600, or in 4/5 of the cases, the test will be negative.

In Figure 34 the eight labels at the end branches include two branches, 1 and 5, in which both test results are positive; $DP_1 P_2$ and $\bar{D}P_1 P_2$. In only one of these, $DP_1 P_2$, do patients actually have the disease.

After a second positive test, the probability that Joe has the disease would be the cases where patients have the disease divided by the total number of cases in which the patient had two positive tests. That is,

$$p(D|P_1 P_2) = \frac{p(DP_1 P_2)}{p(DP_1 P_2) + p(\bar{D}P_1 P_2)} = \frac{4/10(9/10)^2}{4/10(9/10)^2 + 6/10(1/5)^2}$$

$$= \frac{324/1,000}{324/1,000 + 6/250} = \frac{324/1,000}{324/1,000 + 24/1,000} = \frac{324}{348}$$

Instead of a probability of 360/480 or 75 out of 100 after only the first positive test, we now have 324/348 or about 93 out of 100 that he has the disease.

Repeating the test still a third time for people with two positive results (at branches 1 and 5), we can obtain the probabilities of three consecutive positive test results for people with the disease (D) at branch 1 and for people with no disease ($\bar{D}$) at branch 5. These probabilities are:

$$p(DP_1 P_2 P_3) = 4/10(9/10)^3 = 2,916/10,000$$

$$p(\bar{D}P_1 P_2 P_3) = 6/10(1/5)^3 = 6/1,250$$

After a third positive test the probability that Joe has the disease, D, would be:

$$p(D|P_1 P_2 P_3) = \frac{p(DP_1 P_2 P_3)}{p(DP_1 P_2 P_3) + p(\bar{D}P_1 P_2 P_3)} = \frac{2,916/10,000}{2,916/10,000 + 6/1,250}$$

$$= \frac{2,916/10,000}{2,916/10,000 + 48/10,000} = \frac{2,916}{2,964}$$

This is approximately 98 out of 100 that Joe has the disease.

A fourth positive test would make the probability that Joe has the disease:

$$p(D|P_1P_2P_3P_4) = \frac{p(DP_1P_2P_3P_4)}{p(DP_1P_2P_3P_4) + p(\bar{D}P_1P_2P_3P_4)}$$

$$= \frac{26,244/10,000}{26,244/100,000 + 6/6,250}$$

$$= \frac{26,244/100,000}{26,244/100,000 + 96/100,000} = \frac{26,244}{26,340} = 0.996$$

That is a probability larger than 99 out of 100. Joe went to see another doctor.

---

is he honest?

Alex returned from the hospital late one afternoon. His friend Joe was recovering from major surgery. The operation was performed after weeks of concern about the accuracy of the diagnosis. The decision was made after a test administered for the third time confirmed the results of two earlier tests. The uncertainties that attended the weeks of waiting made it very difficult to decide on a course of action. When Alex reached his uncle's home, he found him in one of his philosophical moods. Alex brought up the topic of uncertainty and how relevant information can be used to dispel doubt and enhance our state of knowledge.

will to doubt   "You recall, Alex, we discussed 'The will to doubt' in the past and identified it as an important attitude to problem solving in general. It provides the flexibility that enables us to change our plans in the face of *new information* which is relevant to a problem."

"But does this really mean that we should go around doubting everything and having faith in nothing?" Alex questioned.

"Not at all," his uncle answered. "Let me step back a little to explain. Suppose we consider your friend, Joe. Shortly before Joe went to see the doctor he was feeling fine. At this time the *hypothesis* could be made that Joe did not have disease *D*. This hypothesis was accepted on faith, but with an open mind in the sense of the *will to doubt* principle. That is, if sufficient evidence is received to challenge it, we can reject the hypothesis."

"But how much is sufficient evidence?" asked Alex.

"This, of course, is personal and depends very much on what is at stake," answered his uncle. "Joe did not consider the results of the first test to be sufficient evidence that he had the disease, but after the second and third tests confirmed the results of the first, he rejected the hypothesis that he did not have the disease and accepted the verdict that he did have the disease."

Alex nodded his understanding and said, "So we actually begin with faith in a hypothesis, although we are aware of the possibility that we may be induced by new evidence to reject it."

"Right," replied his uncle. "In fact, if we had to wait for all doubt to be dispelled before we could have faith in something, we could not have faith in anything.

"This is the basis of the scientific method. A hypothesis is made on the basis of initial observations, ideas, and studies, and we might say it is 'accepted' on a tentative basis until sufficient evidence leads to its rejection. So we begin with faith, but with a mind open to the possibility of change in our belief."

Alex tried to summarize: "So the question of how much doubt or how much faith we have in a premise or hypothesis is a matter of degree, and is subjective in nature. The degree of our faith is related to our knowledge and the information at our disposal."

"That's correct, Alex. To incorporate in a model new information that may enhance our faith in a premise (or increase our doubt), we can assign a quantitative value to our state of knowledge. Such an assignment takes the form of a number between zero and one. The value of one represents absolute faith in a premise; a value of zero represents absolute lack of faith in a premise. In either case we leave no room for doubt; it takes as much complete conviction to have absolute faith as it does to have absolute lack of faith. In other words, we can always take a positive statement such as: 'All men are created equal,' and state it in a negative form; 'Not all men are created equal.' Absolute faith in the first statement (value: one) will require the same conviction as absolute lack of faith (value: zero) in the second."

97

"But, Uncle, you once told me that the attitude of the will to doubt suggests that we assign the values of zero and one with great caution, or better yet, keep the options open by assigning values which are very close to one (0.999. . .) or to zero (0.000. . .1) when we have a great deal of relevant and credible information regarding a premise or hypothesis. After all, does any mortal problem solver have perfect knowledge? Can one really have all relevant information with no shadow of doubt regarding its credibility?"

"Man's need to know, his need for faith and will to doubt, and the problems which are a result of these needs, stem from his peculiar cognitive activity which places him between animal and the concept of God. An animal is not capable of cognitive activity as long as it is ignorant of everything, including its own ignorance. The animal will thus make no effort to gain knowledge. At the other end is the concept of a God who has no reason to make an effort because he is all knowing and knows that he knows. Only man, the being between the all-ignorant animal and the all-knowing God, must make an effort to move from ignorance to knowledge because he has the gift of being aware of his ignorance. The greatness of man is that he knows that he does not know, and it is this knowledge, coupled with the need to know, that creates man's problems."

Alex listened attentively and then added, "I recall reading that Descartes began modern philosophy when he claimed that man can doubt everything, but in order to be in a position to doubt everything he must not doubt that he doubts. So I suppose that here is the primitive basic premise of the will to doubt: We cannot doubt that we doubt."

"Yes, Alex. On the other hand I suppose one can argue that instead of placing the emphasis on the will to doubt, we should stress the will to believe. However, the will to believe has promoted historically an attitude that propagated dogma; that stifled free thinking, and suppressed questioning. The will to doubt promotes the desire to find out, to search."

Alex nodded his understanding. As he was mulling over his uncle's words, he got an idea. "Tell me again how you describe the concept of a probability."

Professor Gordian began, "We all have an intuitive concept of probability as related to the outcome of events such as flipping coins or rolling dice. But we also use the term in such sentences as 'It will probably rain tomorrow.'

"Consider, for example, the statements:

The probability is 0.6 that it will rain tomorrow.
The probability is 0.8 that it will rain tomorrow.

It is quite possible that you arrive at the assessment of probabilities about rain by consulting ten weather predictions and taking the ratio of the number of predictions for rain over the total number of predictions. This method is, of course, based on the implicit assumption that each prediction carries the same weight, or equal credibility, as a prediction of rain on the average.

"In the first statement, that the probability is 0.6, there are six predictions out of ten for rain and four for no rain, and in the second statement these numbers are eight and two, respectively.

"The second statement represents a higher state of knowledge or degree of certainty than the first.

"In a similar manner, consider these statements:

The probability of a head in the toss of the coin is 0.5.
The probability of a head in the toss of the coin is 1.0.

"The second statement shows absolute knowledge regarding the outcome of the toss; apparently the coin has a head on each face. In the first statement we bring experience into our assessment because we normally recall coins falling heads half the time. It is interesting to ask people for the probability of a thumbtack falling with the head flat on a table. You will be surprised at the spectrum of numbers between zero and one. Here experience is rather limited, as you yourself have found out.

"Note that an assignment of probability of 1/2 to a statement about *two* alternatives represents the lowest state of knowledge. A number larger than 1/2 indicates that more knowledge has caused us to be closer to certainty in our faith (value of one) in the statement, and a number smaller than 1/2 indicates that additional knowledge has caused us to be closer to certainty in our lack of faith (value of zero) in the statement. The maximum doubt or uncertainty in the truth value of a statement is represented by 1/2. In this case we have insufficient knowledge to be inclined either toward its truth or its falseness. A change of a probability from 1/2 represents new knowledge which dispels some doubt." Professor Gordian drew the diagram shown in Figure 35.

"But then what exactly does this tell me about what a probability is?" queried Alex.

"A probability assignment is a numerical encoding of a state of knowledge," answered Professor Gordian matter of factly.

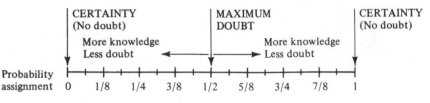

Figure 35. The relationship between probability and doubt in predicting an event.

Alex wrinkled his brow. "That seems different than what you stated earlier. What exactly do you mean by a *state of knowledge*? After all, when I say the probability is 1/2 that a coin will land heads or tails, I profess my knowledge of the coin, and I can flip it many times and show that indeed half the time the coin falls heads. But if I claim a probability of 9/10 that Mr. P will be elected to the Senate, I mean something else. I cannot have Mr. P run for office hundreds of times and keep score of wins and losses."

"This is a very subtle point, Alex. Let us take your examples. Your knowledge of the coin tells you that it will land with heads up 1/2 the time. Your knowledge of the circumstance under which Mr. P is running for office leads you to a statement that he has a probability of 0.9 of winning. The *knowledge* I am talking about is the knowledge of what *will happen* with the coin or with Mr. P, and this knowledge is encoded in the numbers 1/2 and 9/10. Although you can experiment repeatedly to convince yourself about the 1/2 for the coin, and you cannot do so to gain evidence about the 9/10 for Mr. P, you seem to have less doubt about *what will happen* in Mr. P's race for office than in what will happen when you flip the coin."

"I don't think I understand," said Alex, with a puzzled expression.

"Let me try again. Suppose you can receive $1,000 for a correct prediction, and you have a choice between predicting the result of a toss of a coin, or the outcome for Mr. P in his race for the Senate. Which would you choose?"

"I see what you mean." replied Alex with a smile. "I would choose to predict that Mr. P. will win the race, since I think I know more about the outcome of the race than the result from the flip of the coin. The probability of 1/2 for heads and 1/2 for tails represents a state of knowledge with the greatest uncertainty about which of the two events will occur."

Professor Gordian beamed his satisfaction at Alex's understanding. "Let us try another example to emphasize the attitude of the will to doubt.

"Consider this question: 'Is Mr. X an honest man?' What do you think is the likely response of a person who knows Mr. X and has no will to doubt, but wishes to use a probability assignment to assess his state of knowledge?"

"I believe such a person will say: 'Mr. X is honest, and the probability that this statement is true is one. I know the man and no one can tell me something that will make me change my mind.' Or he might say the exact reverse."

Professor Gordian nodded his approval. "What about a person with a will to doubt?"

Alex replied, "Such a person will say: 'Mr. X is honest and the probability is very close to one, say 0.99999, that this statement is true. After all, I base my statement on what I know, and I am the first to admit that I do not know everything. Yet I have learned to have faith, knowing that one cannot wait for all doubt to be dispelled before faith is professed. The probability of 0.99999 rather than one is merely a display of my will to doubt, and through it I profess that I am human and that my knowledge is therefore not complete."

Professor Gordian huried to add, "But wait, Alex, we are not through with the story. There is evidence that Mr. X was seen on weekends, standing in a glass booth in a Las Vegas casino (as shown in Figure 36) playing the following game. As customers enter they can bet one dollar against five house dollars that when the man in the booth flips the dime in his hand, a tail will show. No one forces the customers to play, of course, but in the past six months since the glass booth made its appearance, many made the bet and

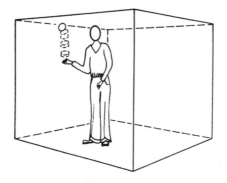

Figure 36. The coin tosser in the glass booth.

all have lost. How will your two people react to this evidence, Alex?"

Alex replied confidently, "The person with no will to doubt will react with the expected dogmatic attitude and claim the evidence to be false. If we offer him a free trip to observe and find out for himself, he will reject the offer, and say that even if the evidence is true, it is not relevant. He has made up his mind and that's it!

"The second person will take a different attitude. He values new evidence, but he wishes to check its credibility, particularly when such a serious matter as the reputation of a man is concerned. He will go to Las Vegas and observe the game to verify the story. How much evidence—in our case, how many coin tosses—he must observe before he will say that the man is dishonest (because he is partner to a dishonest game) will be a matter of individual judgement."

Professor Gordian was obviously pleased with Alex's analysis. "This last point you made is worth emphasizing, Alex. Our education provides us with knowledge which includes a host of tools and a great deal of information in various forms. Our education is also supposed to provide us with the mental habits and tools to learn on our own. This should help us acquire new knowledge when we recognize the need for it, so we can make rational and sound judgments for ourselves when we solve problems. It is the habits and tools of learning and the making of judgments for ourselves, which are the most important. But it is possible that we stifle these habits by a tradition of formalism in education that borders on conveying dogmatic patterns for problem solving."

search for the odd coin

Alex and the Professor were on one of their skiing trips again when Alex remembered the problem of the 12 coins that his friend Joe had asked him to present to the Professor. There are 12 coins identical in shape, with 11 having the same weight and one having a different weight. A balance is provided and the object is to identify the odd coin in three weighings and to establish whether it is lighter or heavier than one of the other coins.

The Professor found a real challenge in thinking about the problem. But the solution was not in sight even after 2 hours of effort.

Alex was sorry he had brought up the problem. He suggested that perhaps he had stated the problem incorrectly, trying to give the Professor a way out. The Professor sensed that Alex was embarrassed for him.

"Look, Alex, just because I advocate the teaching of problem solving does not mean that I have the answers to all problems. The approach to problem solving, the search for solutions, teaches more about problem solving than having the solutions.

"Here, let me share with you my thinking so far. I first started with a similar problem that I remembered. In that problem you have 27 coins, of which one is heavier than the remaining 26 that have identical weights."

Alex interrupted, "But, Professor, in our problem we do not know whether the odd coin is heavier or lighter."

"I know, Alex, but let me simplify the problem first so I can perhaps extract a basic approach which may then be helpful with your problem. So here is how we solve the 27 coins problem. We divide the coins into three groups of nine coins each. We weigh two groups against each other on the balance scales. If they are equal, the heavy coin is with the remaining group. If the balance tips to one side, that side has the group with the odd coin. A single weighing will identify one group of the three as the one containing the odd coin. Now we take this group of nine coins and divide it into three groups of three coins each. By the reasoning we have just used, we can identify in one weighing the group that contains the odd coin. We now separate the three coins of this group and using one more weighing we identify the odd coin as you can see from this sketch." (See Figure 37.)

"What is the general message in the procedure you used with the 27 coins?" asked Alex.

"Well Alex, problem solving can sometimes be approached by a search that involves selective rejection. The more coins you reject as not being the odd one in our problem, the closer you get to the solution. In general, in complex problems when we are in no position to know for sure that we have the best solution, we may have a number of alternatives to consider as potential solutions. The more of these alternatives we reject on the basis of reasonable

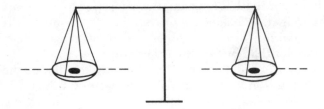

Figure 37. Last weighing. If balance is even, then the odd coin is not on the balance. If the balance tips, the side that tips down has the odd coin.

criteria, the more confidence we have in the solution we finally adopt. In such situations, even when a solution occurs to us on the first try, we should compare it with alternative solutions. The more alternative solutions we reject the more confidence we have in our original solution.

"Remember the testing of a hypothesis in the scientific method? We gain confidence in a hypothesis by rejecting efforts to prove it wrong. The more we reject the more confident we are."

Alex indeed remembered about scientific hypothesis testing. But he was eager to apply the principles to new examples. "Can the idea that problem solving is sometimes a matter of selective rejection be illustrated by other examples?" he asked.

"Let me try one," replied his uncle. "Consider a person arriving at these intersections." The professor took out his pad and pencil and drew some diagrams and labeled them as shown in Figure 38. "Only one of the routes leads to the desired destination, but he does not know which. A genie stationed at each intersection will respond with *yes* or *no* to any question. The answer is always credible, but there is a fixed fee per question. How many questions should the person ask at each intersection?" Figure 39 shows diagrammatically that one question "Is it road 0?" will do for both routes in Figure 38(a). If the answer is "yes," road 0 is correct, and if the answer is "no," then road 1 is correct. Two questions are needed for Figure 38(b). First divide the routes into two equal parts, 0 and 1 versus 2 and 3. The first question is "does the correct route lie in the group containing 0 and 1?" If "yes," then we have reduced the situation to the problem in Figure 38(a) where we have to decide between just two routes. This will take one more question. If the answer is "no," then the correct route lies in the group containing 2 and 3. Our search will still take just one more question for a total of two. For Figure 38(c), we first

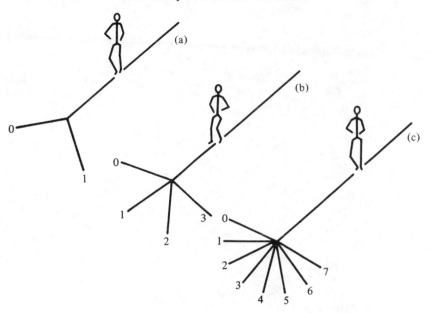

Figure 38. Routes at an intersection: (a) 2 routes: 0, 1; (b) four routes: 0, 1, 2, 3; (c) eight routes: 0, 1, 2, 3, 4, 5, 6, 7, 8.

divide the routes into two equal groups, one containing 0, 1, 2, and 3, and the other containing 4, 5, 6, and 7. Our first question is, "Is the correct route in the group containing 0, 1, 2, and 3?" Either a "yes" or a "no" answer will then reduce the situation to Figure 38(b) where there are only four routes left. This will require two more questions, for a total of three. In general, for 2^n routes, n questions will lead to the correct route. The first question reduces the region of search by a factor of 2; that is, we can reject half of the routes. This is achieved by dividing our uncertainty into 2 equal parts, in the sense that each part has an equal probability of including the solution. Similarly, each successive question reduces the remaining search region by a factor of 2, each time dividing the remaining routes into two groups that have an equal probability of containing the solution. The professor drew the diagrams shown in Figure 39 and continued. "The selective rejection through questions continues to reduce our uncertainty as fewer and fewer routes remain as possible candidates for the solution." This can be illustrated also in the form of a general *decision tree* for questions, which is an abstraction of Figure 39. The Professor drew the diagram of Figure 40.

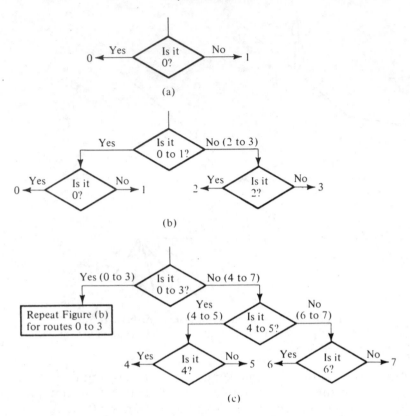

Figure 39. Sequence of n questions to find the correct route out of 2^n routes. (a) Two routes: 0,1; (b) Four routes: 0, 1, 2, 3; (c) eight routes: 0, 1, 2, 3, 4, 5, 6, 7, 8.

"But Professor," Alex protested, "Isn't there a simpler way to go about the process of rejection? Suppose that I were to simply take one alternative at a time and ask if it were the correct route? Suppose there were four different routes and I was trying to find the one correct route. I could simply start with the first route and ask if it were the correct one, and if it didn't turn out to be, I would go on to the next one, and so on. I might be able to get the answer in only one question! You would never be able to do this if you divided the routes in half and asked if the correct route were contained in one half. It would always take two questions to get the answer."

"You are correct, Alex. You would occasionally be able to find

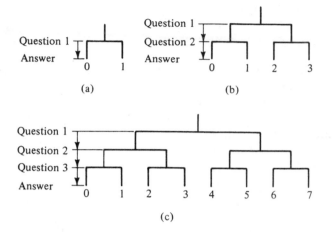

Figure 40. Decision trees, abstractions of Figure 39.
(a) 2^1 routes, 1 question; (b) 2^2 routes, 2 questions;
(c) 2^3 routes, 3 questions.

the correct route in only one question. But sometimes it would take you three questions to get the correct answer. My method guarantees that I could always find the correct route in only two questions."

The Professor put two fingers to his lips and thought intensely for a moment. "In fact, Alex, I can show that the expected value for the number of questions that you would have to ask with your method is greater than two questions!"

Alex's eyes widened. "Really? I'd like to see this."

"Well! I thought you'd never ask!" The Professor grinned and quickly started sketching out a tree diagram to show all of the possibilities for Alex's proposed method. "As you can see from this sketch, after you ask your first question of whether the first route is the correct one, there are two possibilities. You can either get a yes or a no answer. Since there are four routes and only one of them is correct, the probability of you getting a yes is 1/4 and the probability of you getting a no is 3/4. If you do get a yes, you have been lucky and gotten the answer in only one question. But if the answer to your first question is no, you must ask if the second route is the correct one. Since there are three routes left, the probability of a yes is 1/3 that you will get the correct answer in only two questions, and 2/3 that you must go on to ask still another question. If you get a no for your second question, you must then ask if the third route is the correct one. The probability of you getting a yes is now 1/2 since there are only two routes left. If the answer is yes, you know that the third route is the correct one and you have gotten the correct answer in three questions. And even if the answer is no, also with a probability of 1/2, you have still gotten the answer in three questions because the correct route then must be the fourth route. You can now calculate the expected value for the number of questions by your approach."

Alex jumped. "Oh, let me do it!" He grabbed the pencil and paper and started scribbling madly. His work is shown in Figure 41. He quickly thought to himself, "I need to multiply the probability of finding the correct route in a given number of questions by that number of questions, and sum over all possible numbers of questions. There can be either one question, two questions, or three questions. I'll start with one question. The probability of getting the correct answer in one question is 1/4, so I'll take 1/4 times one as the first term in computing the expected value. Now to get the probability of finding the correct route in two questions I must multiply down the tree diagram, because I am considering the probability of not finding the correct route on the first question, and then finding it on the second. That will give me 3/4 times 1/3.

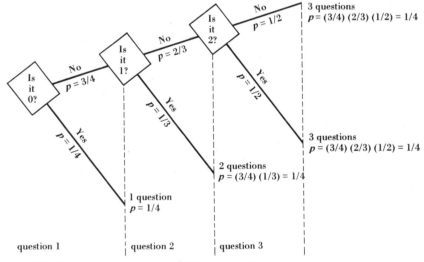

expected value of number of questions to find correct route =
$1/4(1) + (3/4)(1/3)(2) + (3/4)(2/3)(1/2)(3) + (3/4)(2/3)(1/2)(3) = 2\ 1/4$

Figure 41. Alex's calculations to find the expected number of questions for his questioning technique.

If I take this probability and multiply it by the number of questions, two, I will get the second term in my summation for the expected value. Now for the probability of finding the correct route in three questions, I must multiply down the tree again. For not getting the correct answer on questions one and two, I must multiply 3/4 times 2/3. Now to get a yes on question three I multiply by 1/2, which gives me 3/4 times 2/3 times 1/2, which is the probability of one way of getting the correct answer in three questions. So 3/4 times 2/3 times 1/2 times three will be the next term in my expected value equation. But I will also find the correct route with three questions if the answer to the third question is no. That also has a probability of 3/4 times 2/3 times 1/2. So the last term in finding the expected value is 3/4 times 2/3 times 1/2 times three. Now all I have to do is to add up all of these terms. Let's see."

Alex continued scribbling and then exclaimed, "The expected value is 2 1/4 questions!" Then a look of puzzlement came over his face. "Hey, how can I ask 1/4 of a question?"

"You can't, Alex," explained Professor Gordian. "All that your expected value means is that on the average it will take you 2 1/4 questions. On any given try, it will take you either one, two, or three questions. The expected value of 2.25 indicates that quite often, in fact half the time, it will take you three questions to find the correct route. But if you will recall, my method of halving guarantees that I will find the correct route in only two questions. So on the average, my method is quicker."

"Ah, now I see what you are talking about. By halving the uncertainty with each question, you get the correct answer by the fastest method on the average."

"Quite right. Now if we refer back to Figure 40, we can agree that the answer to each question represents the same amount of information.

"After all, in each case the domain of search is reduced by a factor of 2. In each case we get a response of *yes* or *no*. On the basis of this common unit of measurement, we conclude that n units of information are required to find the one correct route out of 2^n routes."

"You once told me that measurement of information is related to probability," Alex interjected.

"Yes, it is. If we consider the two routes of Figure 38(a), with no knowledge as to which is more likely to be correct, we assign each a probability of 1/2 of being the one we seek. This reflects our state of maximum doubt or uncertainty. For four routes, we assign each an equal probability of 1/4, and for 2^n routes, $1/2^n$ each. The larger the number of routes, the smaller is the probability of any single route being the correct one, and the greater our uncertainty. The amount of information required to dispel uncertainty increases as uncertainty increases."

"How is all this related to the coin weighing problem?" asked Alex.

"In the routes problem, each question enabled us to reject one half of the routes. In the case of the 27 coins, we divide the field of search, or our uncertainty of where the odd coin is, into three parts, each with an equal probability of 1/3 of containing the odd coin. Because of the special nature of a balance scale, we can reject two out of three parts following each weighing, which corresponds to one question in the route problem.

"Now returning to the 12 coins, can we employ the same approach? Well, intuitively I believe we can, but knowledge of the principle does not guarantee that its application is going to be easy or simple in every case. The 12 coins problem seems to be a very difficult case.

"Suppose we divide the 12 coins into 3 groups of 4 coins each. Let's label the groups A, B, C."

"OK," said Alex, eager to help, "Let me take 12 pieces of paper to represent the coins and identify each coin in each group by a label written on it. The coins in group A will have labels, a_1, a_2, a_3, and a_4, respectively. Now how do we proceed with the process of selective rejection by dividing the uncertainty into three equal parts each time?"

Professor Gordian continued deliberately, "Step 1: Place two groups on the balance scale, one group on each side. Since each group is equally likely to contain the odd coin (with a probability of one third), it doesn't matter which two groups are placed on the balance. So suppose we place group A against B. What are the possible results?"

Professor Gordian answered his own question. "Case 1-C: The scale does not tip. So we reject groups A and B and concentrate on C as the group that has the odd coin.

"Case 1-A or 1-B: The scale tips to one side. We reject C. A or B contains the odd coin. But how would you proceed from here? Case 1-C left us with four coins and cases 1-A or 1-B each leaves us with eight!"

Both Alex and his uncle were quiet for a moment. Then Professor Gordian continued, "Step 2 for Case 1-C: This is difficult, but let's start with Case 1-C. From our experience with the balance in the 27 coins problem, we know that in a single weighing we can identify one odd coin in a group of three coins provided we know whether the odd coin is heavier or lighter than the other two. We have four coins in group C, and we have yet to establish whether the odd coin is lighter or heavier. We have only two weighings left since we've already used one of the three. Suppose we consider breaking the group of four coins into two groups: a group of three (c_1, c_2, c_3) on the one hand, and c_4 on the other. Note that there is as much uncertainty when we know that a group of three coins is heavier or lighter than a group of three normal coins, as there is when we know that a single coin, c_4, is the odd one but don't know whether c_4 is heavier or lighter. In each case one more weighing is required.

"Also note that the sequence of weighings is very important. To begin, we take the group consisting of $c_1 c_2$ and c_3 and place it on the scale against a group of normal coins, say $a_1 a_2 a_3$. *If the scale doesn't tip,* then c_4 is the odd coin. If we next place c_4 on the balance against any other normal coin, we will then know whether the odd coin, c_4, is heavier or lighter. On the other hand, if the balance tips when we weigh $c_1 c_2$ and c_3 against the normal group, then we know that $c_1 c_2 c_3$ is the group containing the odd coin. The odd coin is heavier if the balance tips to the side of $c_1 c_2 c_3$, and the odd coin is lighter if the balance tips the other way. In either case one more weighing will identify the odd coin. So we achieve the goal in a total of three weighings."

"Why was the sequence of weighing important?" asked Alex.

"If we were to start with c_4 we could be lucky and in one weighing against a normal coin, say a_4, establish whether it is heavier or lighter—if indeed it happens to be the odd coin. This would yield the solution in a total of two weighings. But suppose we're not so lucky. Suppose c_4 balances a_4. Then we know the odd coin is in the group $c_1 c_2 c_3$, which would require two more weighings for a total of four to isolate the odd coin. The sequence I originally described is the *'sure-thing'* approach that guarantees the solution in a total of three weighings. But it rules out the good fortune of achieving it in two, just as it avoids the misfortune of requiring more than three weighings."

Alex stopped his uncle. "Let me think about that. I could pick, say c_2, weigh it against a normal coin and discover by chance that it is heavier."

"Yes, continued Professor Gordian, "But what if you aren't lucky? We want a procedure that guarantees the solution in no more than three weighings. It is similar to the routes problem we discussed earlier. I could be lucky and ask the genie one question, say, 'Is it route 12?,' and find the one correct route out of 16. But such a question divides the uncertainty unevenly into 1/16 and 15/16 instead of dividing it equally into 8/16 and 8/16 as in our 'sure-thing' approach, which guarantees the answer in four questions. Singling out one route against all remaining routes in each question may lead to the answer in one question, or in as many as fifteen."

"But couldn't we achieve what you just did by dividing group C into two groups: c_1, c_2 and c_3, c_4?" asked Alex.

"I tried that, Alex, but I couldn't find a way to *guarantee* a solution in *no more* than the two additional weighings that are left at that point."

"Well how about the principle of dividing the uncertainty? How did it actually work here, Professor?"

Professor Gordian explained, "When we put the group of three coins, $c_1 c_2$ and c_3, on the scale against $a_1 a_2$ and a_3, there are three equally probable results. The balance may tip to the right, tip to the left, or remain level. Each has a probability of 1/3.

"When I tried to place c_1 and c_2 against c_3 and c_4, there were only two possibilities—the scale tips right or left. The odd coin must be on one side or the other."

Alex attempted to summarize, "So the key concept here is that each weighing must lead to three equally probable results, so that following each weighing we can reject the two that don't occur."

"Well said, Alex," Professor Gordian approved. He then went on: "We still have Case 1-A or 1-B, when the scale tips in the first weighing. This leaves us with eight coins and not four as in Case 1-C. Can we still find the odd coin in no more than two additional weighings?

"That's where I am stuck, but as we are talking about it, I believe I see a way. If the scale tips to one side, say with Group B, we should use what we did earlier with the group of four. Namely, we can find a partition of the coins so that we have three states possible. The balance becomes level, or the balance remains unchanged, or it tips the other way. Whatever the result, the coins rejected in this weighing process should leave us with a need for only one additional weighing."

Alex suggested, "Perhaps we can use some of the normal coins of Group C."

"Excellent," replied Professor Gordian. "Yes, I think we are on the right track. Let's return to Cases 1-A or 1-B with Group C rejected. Suppose the balance tips in the first weighing (as shown in Figure 42). Following what we did earlier, we can use the second weighing to determine whether a group of three coins $a_1 a_2 a_3$ or $b_1 b_2 b_3$, respectively, is heavier or lighter than a normal group $c_1 c_2 c_3$, or whether one of the remaining coins a_4 or b_4 is the odd one."

Alex, trying to help out as much as he could added, "But since you said that our approach consists of dividing the uncertainty into three equal parts, we must arrange the coins to permit the balance to assume three equally probable states, given what we know. Thus, after we rearrange groups of coins (in Figure 42), the balance may remain in the same state, it may tip the other way, or it may move to a level position."

"How are we going to do that?" queried Professor Gordian. Then almost immediately he answered himself. "Alex, I've got it! I believe I do. . . . Let me try it. In order to achieve the three possible states you mentioned, on the left side we replace group $a_1 a_2 a_3$ with $c_1 c_2 c_3$, and exchange a_4 with b_4 to permit the three possible states of the balance shown in Figure 43."

Alex looked on thoughtfully. "You have the two groups of three coins, $a_1 a_2 a_3$ and $b_1 b_2 b_3$, and the single coins, a_4 and b_4, identified as I thought. But will this arrangement do the trick?"

"Why don't you reason this out by looking at these drawings (Figures 42 and 43)?" asked Professor Gordian.

By now Alex was really intrigued and was thinking carefully

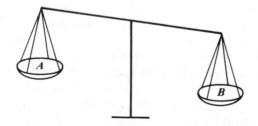

Figure 42. Possible outcome on the first weighing.

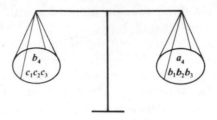

(b) Becomes level

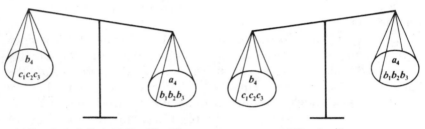

(a) Remains as in first weighing (Fig. 42)   (c) Tips the other way

Figure 43. Professor Gordian's proposed solution to one outcome in the 12 coin problem.

about the problem. "O.K. Let me try, but slowly. If the result is this (Figure 43(a)), then replacing $a_1 a_2 a_3$ by normal coins $c_1 c_2 c_3$ and exchanging a_4 and b_4 had no influence on the state of the balance. Therefore all of these are normal coins and we can conclude that $b_1 b_2 b_3$ contains the odd coin and it is heavier. If like this (Figure 43(b)), we conclude that all coins on the balance are normal, and the replaced group $a_1 a_2 a_3$ contains the odd coin and it is lighter (see Figure 42).

"Here (Figure 43(c)) the odd coin cannot be in the group $a_1 a_2 a_3$ which was removed, because then the balance would contain only normal coins and would be level (as in Figure 43(b)). The odd coin cannot be in $b_1 b_2 b_3$, because otherwise all the other coins would be normal and the balance would remain like this (Figure 42). So, the odd coin must be either a_4 or b_4. So, (from Figure 42 and Figure 43(c)), we can conclude that either a_4 is the odd coin and is lighter than a normal coin, or b_4 is the odd coin and is heavier than a normal coin.

"In each of the states ([(a), (b), or (c)] in Figure 43), one additional weighing will complete the solution to the problem."

"Well done, Alex," stated Professor Gordian, looking exceedingly pleased. "Were you aware of the fact that you were using *selective* rejection in your reasoning following each of the results of the weighing shown here (Figure 43)?"

"Come to think about it, Professor, you are right, but I really wasn't aware of it while I was doing it."

"Well, we got it. Doesn't it feel great?" asked Professor Gordian grinning broadly.

"You got it, not we," retorted Alex in a jovial manner, obviously very pleased himself.

"Oh no, Alex, I mean *we*. The last part only came to me when I was trying to explain to you how I got to the point where I was stuck. You reminded me of the normal coins in Group *C,* and that helped. Then when you reminded me of what I had said regarding three equally probable states in the weighing, I focused on possible arrangements of groups of three along with single coins. It was this which gave me the insight for the last step. So it helps to talk about the problem when we are stuck. It's more fun also."

"I'd better write down the solution so I will not forget. Boy, I can't wait to show Joe." Alex sparkled at his newfound wisdom. "Do you have another simple example of the method of dividing the uncertainty into equal parts? It sounds so general and useful."

Professor Gordian thought for a moment and came up with what Alex had asked for. "Here is another example. Suppose we have eight marbles of different colors in a coffee cup. If I draw one marble, how many yes–no type questions (binary questions) do you have to ask to establish the color of the marble I have?"

"This is the same as the eight different routes, so I need three questions," replied Alex quickly.

"Correct. But now let me put four red marbles, two blue, one green, and one white in the coffee cup. Now how many binary questions, must you ask?"

"I suppose three since we still have eight marbles," replied Alex.

"But I am concerned only with color, not with a unique label as to whether it is red$_1$, red$_2$, red$_3$, red$_4$, etc." added Professor Gordian.

"I know, but I still think it will take three questions to guarantee that I will not end up asking more questions, as may happen if I am not careful with the sequence of questions."

"Excellent, Alex. Tell me what your questions would be."

Alex began, "First I divide the uncertainty into two groups, so that one question will reject one group. One group will be the four red marbles and the other group will contain the other four marbles. Each group has a probability of 1/2 of including the marble you have drawn. So the first question will be: 'Is it red?' If the answer is 'yes,' I get the answer in one question. If the answer is 'no' then I divide the remaining four marbles into two groups, each with equal probability of containing the one you have chosen. Now I can reject one of the groups by a single question. So the second question could be: 'Is it blue?' If the answer is 'yes,' I have the answer in two questions. If it is 'no,' one more question will do it. So you see, I may need three questions."

"I'm impressed, Alex. But let me take a slightly different example. Suppose we have seven red marbles and one blue marble. Do you still need three questions?"

"I see your point, Professor. I can do it in one question. But that's true because we have two colors and not three or four. If we had one color, I would need no questions."

"Excellent point," complimented Professor Gordian. "My examples are not always appropriate. Here is what I am trying to say. If we had eight different colors, each color would have a probability of 1/8 of being selected.

"Asking the first question by the method of dividing the uncertainty, we would say: 'Is it one of the first four colors?' Suppose the answer to the first question is yes. Then the second question becomes: 'Is it the first or second color?' Suppose the response to the second question is yes. Then the third question becomes: 'Is it the first color?' The answer to the third question establishes the color of the chosen marble.

"We could not have the final answer in the first or second question regardless of whether the response was 'yes' or 'no.' We were left with more than a single color. So we had to ask the three questions. Again, we could be lucky to ask one question about one color at a time and get the answer after one question. But with no luck, we may end up with as many as seven questions, with all accompanied by 'no.'"

"I believe I see something," said Alex. "You mean that when the probabilities of all the events are the same, then we have the greatest uncertainty. But when we aggregate outcomes with the events having unequal probabilities, we have less uncertainty. But how is this used in the case of the eight marbles?"

"Well," answered Professor Gordian, when we aggregate the outcomes into the event red (R) with four marbles, the event blue (B) with two marbles, and the events green (G) and white (W) with one marble each, we have unequal probabilities.

$$p(R) = 1/2, \quad p(B) = 1/4, \quad p(G) = 1/8, \quad p(W) = 1/8$$

"Yes, but I used this information and still required three questions. So why should I be less uncertain?" asked Alex.

"Remember the concept of *expected value*, Alex? The three questions represent a *maximum number*, or an upper bound. You will not need all three every time you play this guessing game with me."

"You mean I can treat the number of questions as some sort of 'reward' and calculate the expected value?"

"Exactly, except we should call each question a 'payment' instead of a reward."

"I get it. I can even get away with one question if I am lucky, and still not put in jeopardy the maximum of 3 questions in the worst case."

"What is the probability that you will get away with one question?" queried Professor Gordian.

"As often as red (*R*) can happen, 4/8 or 1/2," answered Alex.

"I think you can do the rest on your own. Try a tree," suggested Professor Gordian. Alex started to draw the tree of Figure 44. "The tree must represent the outcomes of my three questions. More exactly, it must represent the probabilities of one question, two questions, and the maximum of three questions, so I can calculate the expected value of the number of questions.

"We have for the expected number of questions:

$$(4/8) \ 1 + 4/8 \times (2/4) \ 2 + 4/8 \times 2/4 \times (1/2) \ 3 + 4/8 \times 2/4 \times (1/2) \ 3$$

$$= (1/2) \ 1 + (1/4) \ 2 + (1/8) \ 3 + (1/8) \ 3$$

$$= 1 \ \ 3/4 \text{ questions.}$$

Professor Gordian summarized Alex's work. "So on the average, you will ask 1 3/4 questions each time you have to establish the color of the marble. For each real situation you will ask either one, two, or three questions with probabilities of 1/2, 1/4, and 1/4 respectively, as your tree shows. But if you proceeded with your sequence of questions, say in 100 situations in which I draw a marble, on the average you will ask 175 questions. Now how does this compare with the case of equal probabilities for, say, four colors?"

Alex answered, "If we have two marbles of each color, *R*, *B*, *G*, and *W* then the probabilities are 1/4 for each color. We need two questions, or 200 questions in 100 situations. This is more than the number of questions we need, on the average, when the four

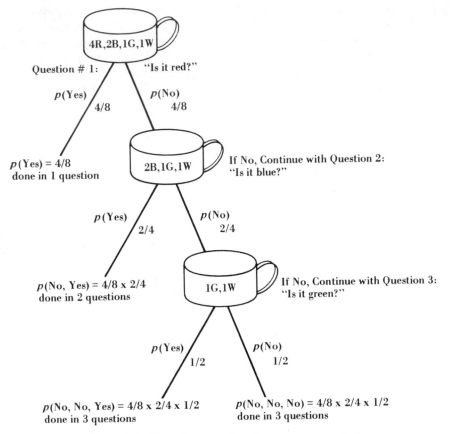

Question # 1: "Is it red?"

p(Yes) / 4/8 p(No) 4/8

p(Yes) = 4/8
done in 1 question

2B,1G,1W

If No, Continue with Question 2:
"Is it blue?"

p(Yes) / 2/4 p(No) 2/4

p(No, Yes) = 4/8 x 2/4
done in 2 questions

1G,1W

If No, Continue with Question 3:
"Is it green?"

p(Yes) / 1/2 p(No) 1/2

p(No, No, Yes) = 4/8 x 2/4 x 1/2
done in 3 questions

p(No, No, No) = 4/8 x 2/4 x 1/2
done in 3 questions

Figure 44. Tree diagram for the outcomes of the colored marble problem.

colors have the unequal probabilities of 1/2, 1/4, 1/8, 1/8. So we are most uncertain in the case of equal probabilities for the events of interest, and we need more questions to dispel more doubt."

"That is correct Alex," said Professor Gordian. "You may be interested in an application of all this. You noticed in your tree that R was identified in one question, B in two, but G and W in three. The larger the probability of the event, the smaller the number of questions.

"In 1838, Samuel F. B. Morse (1791–1872) devised his famous code using this idea. To keep the expected number of code symbols that must be transmitted small, he gave short codes to letters of high frequency and longer ones to the less frequent letters. He estimated the various frequencies of the letters by counting the number of type letters in the bins of a printing shop. Thus 'e,' the most frequent letter in English, has the shortest code, a dot. Each symbol may be considered equivalent to a question in our earlier discussion."

Alex perked up. "This is really interesting. I never thought that probability, information, uncertainty, and expected value can go beyond games of chance in Las Vegas. Perhaps I could have identified applications in business if I had tried, but to relate it to English and the Morse Code makes the subject very relevant to our most basic model of communication, our language."

Later that evening, when Alex was taking a study break, he summarized in his intellectual diary the things he had learned from Professor Gordian in the past few days.

SUMMARY

1/ A probability is a number between zero and one inclusive, that forms a measure of uncertainty. There are at least three different, but related, definitions:

a/ (Subjective definition) Probability is a numerical encoding of a state of belief. A probability of zero means that you have complete faith that some event will not occur, and a probability of one means that you have complete faith that an event will occur. Probabilities between zero and one represent intermediate degrees of belief.

b/ (Objective definition) This definition assumes that it is possible to make repeated observations of the outcome of some situation; e.g., as in repeatedly flipping a thumbtack. The probability of a particular attribute occurring is the number of outcomes with that attribute divided by the total number of outcomes in question.

c/ (Another objective definition) This definition is based on the assumption that events are composed of some number of equally likely outcomes, e.g., in rolling a die. You can

119

assume that the faces are equally likely to show up. This assumption obviates making repeated observations of the results of an experiment, as is necessary in definition (b). The probability of some particular event is the number of outcomes composing that event divided by the total number of outcomes.

2/ The different definitions of probability are related by experience. We learn to expect an outcome in proportion to its relative frequency of occurrence, and where applicable, this relative frequency of occurrence is determined by the ratio of favorable equally likely outcomes to the total number of outcomes.

3/ Odds are another way of quantifying uncertainty. Odds are expressed as the number of outcomes in which some event occurs to the number of outcomes in which that event does not occur. Thus if the odds of an event are a to b, then its probability is $\dfrac{a}{a+b}$.

4/ Expected value refers to the average amount of payoff that occurs on each trial of some uncertain situation. It can be calculated from the formula

$$EV = \Sigma P(E)V(E)$$

5/ A fair game is one in which the expected value is zero.

6/ Independent events are events that do not influence one another; i.e., the outcome of one event does not affect the outcome of the other.

7/ A conditional probability is the probability of an event occurring under the condition that some other event has already occurred. The conditional probability of A given B is written $P(A|B)$.

8/ If A and B are independent, then

$$P(A|B) = P(A)$$

9/ The multiplicative rule can be used to calculate the probability of two events occurring together. The probability of A and B occurring together is given by

$$P(A \cap B) = P(A)P(B|A)$$

10/ Mutually exclusive events are events that cannot occur together. (Thus, mutually exclusive events are not independent.) If A and B are mutually exclusive, and if we know that event A has occurred, then we know that event B cannot have occurred at the same time. The occurrence of A has influenced the occurrence of B.

11/ The additive rule can be used to calculate the probability of one or the other (or both) of two mutually exclusive events occurring. The probability of A or B occurring, given that A and B are mutually exclusive, is given by

$$P(A \cup B) = P(A) + P(B)$$

12/ If events are mutually exclusive and *exhaustive,* that is, if the specified events are the only possible occurrences in a given situation, then the sum of their respective probabilities must equal one.

13/ The additive and multiplicative rules can be used in conjunction with tree diagrams. You can multiply probabilities down a tree to get the probability that outcomes represented at different levels of the tree will occur together. You can add probabilities across a tree to get the probability of the occurrence of one or the other of several mutually exclusive events. If the branches under a node of a tree represent mutually exclusive and exhaustive outcomes, then the probabilities associated with these branches must sum to one.

14/ Frequencies of events, or associated probabilities, can be represented in tables as well as in trees. Conditional probabilities can be derived by dividing cell frequencies by row or column totals, and joint probabilities can be derived by dividing cell frequencies by the total number of observations. Probability trees can be constructed from frequency tables starting with either row or column classifications.

15/ The will to doubt requires that we accept and reject hypotheses on a tentative basis only and remain flexible to the input of new information. It also implies that we should not assign probabilities of zero or one to the truth or falseness of propositions. We can assign values very close to zero or one, but our reluctance to assign values of exactly zero or one reflects our willingness to keep an open mind. The assignment of zero or one reflects a dogmatic desire to ignore new information.

16/ With two alternatives, maximum uncertainty between the alternatives is reflected by a probability assignment of $1/2$ to each alternative. With n alternatives, maximum uncertainty is reflected by the assignment of $1/n$ to each alternative. The closer the probability assignment is to zero or one, the more knowledge is implied, and the closer the probability assignment is to $1/n$, the less knowledge is implied.

17/ In distinguishing which of several alternatives is correct in a situation where new information can be obtained only by asking yes or no questions (or by an equivalent method), the optimal strategy is to divide the uncertainty into equal parts for each question. This means dividing the alternatives into groups, each of which has an equal probability of containing the correct alternative.

While other strategies may occasionally allow detection of the correct alternative in fewer questions, the optimal strategy guarantees the use of the minimal number of questions *on the average*. That is, the expected value of the number of questions is minimal.

PROBLEMS

1/ Get a thumbtack and flip it 100 times. Record the number of times the tack lands with the point up. What is the probability of the tack landing with point up? What definition of probability did you use?

2/ Make an estimate of the probability that it will rain tomorrow in your area. Make an estimate of the probability that your favorite candidate will win the next presidential election. What definitions of probability did you use?

3/ The diagram in Figure 45 illustrates the 52 possible outcomes of drawing one card from a deck of cards. Use this diagram to determine the answers to the following questions. What definition of probability did you use?

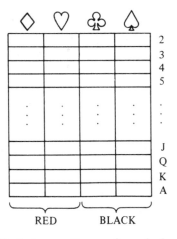

Figure 45. Outcome diagram for a deck of cards.

a/ $P(\text{spade}) = ?$
b/ $P(\text{queen}) = ?$
c/ $P(\text{spade} \cap \text{queen}) = ?$
    Hint: Count to determine the answer. The multiplicative rule can be used, but since there is only one draw of the cards the idea of a conditional probability must be interpreted

in a different manner than if there had been two draws.

d/ $P(\text{spade} \cup \text{queen}) = ?$

Hint: Count to determine the answer. Can you use the additive rule here? Why?

e/ $P(\text{four}) = ?, P(\text{five}) = ?$

f/ $P(\text{four} \cap \text{five}) = ?$

g/ $P(\text{four} \cup \text{five}) = ?$

4/ A deck of cards contains ten cards numbered one to ten.

a/ What is the probability of drawing two cards whose sum is ten?

b/ What is the probability of drawing two cards whose sum is ten if the number five card is removed from the deck?

5/ In Problem 4a, what are the odds of selecting two cards whose sum is five?

6/ If the odds of you winning a race are five to one, what is the probability that you will win?

7/ Indicate whether the following events are independent or not, and whether they are mutually exclusive or not.

a/ drawing an ace from a shuffled deck and rolling a six on a die.

b/ drawing an ace from a deck, replacing it and reshuffling, and then drawing another ace.

c/ you having a traffic accident and it is raining in your area.

d/ the temperature being over $100°F$ ($38°C$) and it is snowing.

e/ drawing an ace and drawing a red card on the same draw.

8/ You are rooting for your favorite basketball team. Over the past season you have determined that the probability of your team leading at half time is 2/3, and that the probability that the team goes on to win given that they led at half time is 2/3. If the team is not leading at half time, the probability that the team goes on to win is only 1/4.

a/ What is the probability that the team will lead at half time and then go on to win?

b/ What is the probability that the team does not lead at half time?

c/ What is the probability that the team does not win given that it is not leading at half time?

d/ What is the probability that the team will not lead at half time and will then go on and not win?

e/ What is the probability that the team wins?

f/ What is the probability that the team loses?

9/ Earthquakes occur at a particular location at the rate of one a month. A team of geologists has determined that the probability of an earthquake of magnitude M or greater is 0.3. What is the probability that, in a four-month period, there will be exactly one earthquake of magnitude M or greater?

10/ Consider the following game. If you roll a one or two on a fair die, you win $2. If you roll a three or four, you lose $1. If you roll a five or six, you lose 50¢. What is the expected value of the game?

11/ Consider the following game. First you roll a die. If a one, two, three, or four comes up, you flip a coin. If a five or a six comes up, you pay $1. If you flip the coin and it comes up heads, you win $3. If it is tails, you pay $1. What is a fair price to pay for this game?

12/ In the game of Keno, as played in Las Vegas, 20 numbers out of 80 are picked at random by the house. The rules of the game allow the player to pick one to 15 of the 80 numbers. The player wins varying amounts, depending on how many numbers were chosen and how many of these numbers are among the 20 picked by the house.

Suppose a player decides to select only one number out of the 80. He receives $1.80 if his number is among the 20 picked by the house and receives nothing if his number is not among the 20.

a/ What is the expected value of this player's strategy?

b/ If it costs 60¢ to play this game, how much should the player expect to win (lose) per game in the long run?

13/ One hundred people have tickets for a certain raffle. Twenty tickets are selected at random. Ten win $7 each, and the other ten win free tickets for a second raffle identical to the first. The remaining 80 ticket holders get nothing. What is the expected value of this raffle?

14/ In a quiz game that consists of two stages, the contestant has three alternatives at each stage. These alternatives and their consequences are:

a/ Answers hard question → correct → His money is quadrupled.
→ wrong → Loses all his money except $100 consolation prize and is out of game.

b/ Answers easy question → correct → Money is doubled.
→ wrong → Loses all money except $100 consolation prize and is out of game.

c/ Does not answer the question → Goes on to next stage.

Suppose a contestant starts with $100 and has probabilities of 0.35 and 0.15 of correctly answering an easy and hard question, respectively. Assuming he is equally likely to select a hard question, an easy question, or abstain, find the probability that he will end up with

a/ $100
b/ $400
c/ $1600

15/ Mr. K has to travel from Washington to Saigon via Paris. The trip from Washington to Paris takes 5 hours with a probability of 0.1 for a delay, and from Paris to Saigon it takes 12 hours with a probability of 0.3 for a delay.

a/ Find the probability that Mr. K will reach Saigon within 17 hours.

b/ Find the probability that he will not reach Saigon within 17 hours.

SHOULD YOU SEE ANOTHER DOCTOR?

16/ In a community of 1000 voters, there are 600 Democrats and 400 Republicans. It is known that in an election in which all 1000 people voted, 20% of the Democrats voted Republican. It is also known that the probability that a Republican voted Republican was 0.9.

a/ Set up a 2 X 2 table to summarize the given data. Fill in all of the cells with the correct frequency values.

b/ If we speak to a citizen who voted Republican, what is the probability that this citizen is a Democrat?

c/ If we speak to a Democrat, what is the probability that this citizen voted Republican?

d/ What is the probability that a Democrat voted Democrat? That a Republican voted Republican?

e/ Who won the election?

17/ Assume that 1000 people take a diagnostic test for cancer with the following properties: Given that a person has cancer, the test is positive (i.e., it indicates that the person has cancer) with a probability of 0.95. Given that a person does not have cancer, the test is negative with a probability of 0.90. Assume that five people out of the 1000 have cancer.

a/ Set up the data in a 2 X 2 table. Fill in all of the cells with the correct frequency values.

b/ Make a tree diagram from your table. Start the tree with the classification "has cancer—does not have cancer" and end it with the classification "positive test—negative test"

c/ Make another tree diagram from your table, but this time start it with "positive test—negative test" and end it with "has cancer—does not have cancer."

d/ Find the probability that a person with a positive test actually has cancer.

e/ Assume that a person takes the diagnostic test described here. After getting a positive result on this test, he goes and takes another independent test with the same sort of probabilities as this test. Suppose he gets another positive result. What is the probability that he has cancer?

f/ Suppose the person in (e/) takes another similar test and gets still another positive test. What is now the probability that he has cancer?

IS HE HONEST

18/ You are trying to determine whether or not Mr. X is honest. Suppose you have just met him and you have absolutely no information to go on.

a/ What probability value would you assign to the statement "Mr. X is honest"? Why?

b/ Now suppose that you have watched Mr. X making bets on the outcome of flipping a coin he has taken out of his pocket. Mr. X has always bet on heads and has won ten out of ten tries. Intuitively, what probability value would you now assign to the statement, "Mr. X is honest"? What if Mr. X had just won 100 out of 100 tosses?

c/ Set up a tree diagram to determine exactly what probability you should assign to the statement, "Mr. X is honest," after he has won ten out of ten tosses. (Hint: Start out the tree diagram with the possibilities "Mr. X is honest" and "Mr. X is dishonest." Assume that if Mr. X is honest he is using a fair coin, and if he is dishonest he is using a two-headed coin. Calculate the probability that Mr. X is honest given that he has just tossed ten heads on ten tosses.)

d/ Suppose you initially had complete confidence in Mr. X's honesty, but still preserved the will to doubt. You assigned the probability value of 0.999 to the statement "Mr. X is honest." Now suppose he won ten out of ten tosses. What is your new probability that Mr. X is honest, given ten heads on ten tosses?

e/ Now suppose that you had initially had complete confidence in Mr. X's honesty, but had not preserved the will to doubt and had assigned the probability value of one to the statement, "Mr. X is honest." Suppose he had just won ten out of ten tosses. What is your new probability assignment? Is this different from the result in (d/)? Why?

19/ Suppose you are faced with eight different routes at an intersection as Figure 46(a) below. Each route has an equal probability of being the correct one.

a/ What strategy should you use to find the correct route by asking the least number of questions, on the average?

b/ What is the expected number of questions that must be asked if you follow your above strategy?

c/ If you were instead to start with one route and ask if that were the correct route and then proceed to do the same for each of the remaining routes until you found the correct one, what is the expected value of this strategy?

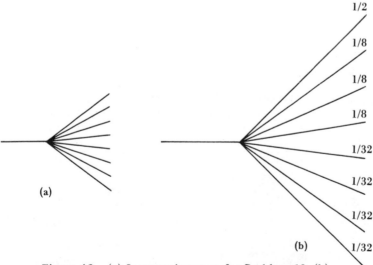

(a)

(b)

1/2
1/8
1/8
1/8
1/32
1/32
1/32
1/32

Figure 46. (a) Intersection map for Problem 19. (b) Intersection map for Problem 20.

20/ Suppose you were faced with the eight different routes shown in Figure 46(b), with the unequal probabilities given.

a/ What is the minimum expected value strategy here?

b/ What is the expected number of questions that must be asked with the above strategy?

c/ If you start your questions with the route of highest probability and ask whether or not this is the correct one, and then proceed with the other routes in order of decreasing probability, what is the expected number of questions that must be asked? What if you proceeded in the same way but started with the lowest probability routes and proceeded on to the higher probability routes in order?

4

Introduction to Decision Making

Professor Gordian was sitting on his front porch sipping from a tall glass of iced tea and watching the hummingbirds flitting and hovering about his homemade feeder when Alex came strolling by.

"Professor! I had hoped that I would find you at home. I need your advice on something. Do you have a while to talk?"

"Surely, Alex. Come on up and have a seat. Can I get you anything to drink?"

"No thanks." Alex walked over to the porch swing and sat opposite his uncle. He looked up at the hummingbirds and a sheepish grin settled on his face. "I'm going to get a new car."

Professor Gordian turned to Alex and smiled. "Good for you, Alex. It's about time you did something about that rattletrap that you've been driving around in for so long."

Alex dropped his jaw in surprise and suddenly brightened up. "Gee, I sort of expected a lecture on withholding judgment and getting the whole picture and having to justify my decision as compared to all other alternatives. I had it all worked out, though. I mean everything I was going to say, such as having a new car is such a great feeling. I've never had a new car, where the paint doesn't look like it should be on an old barn and where there is a warranty and all. I wouldn't have to worry about someone else's hassles with a used car, and I wouldn't have to worry about what else would go wrong if I fixed my old car. I've gotten really excited about a new car."

"Well, Alex, there is nothing to be embarrassed about in wanting to get a new car. After all, no one else can decide what *you* want for you. You have your own values and you have to satisfy them. In fact, it is often a blessing when you know what you want. Then the only problem is getting whatever it is."

"Yes, that's true, but I've only solved part of my problem with my decision to get a new car. The trouble is that I don't know what type of new car to get. I could get another van, which would be great because of my pizza delivery job and because it is so convenient for camping, but I worry about the fuel consumption. The price of gas is getting outrageous. I could get a compact car which would get better gas mileage and be easier to maneuver in the city, but it would be a drag for camping, especially in the rain. I think what worries me most is that I fear that the price of gasoline is going to go sky high soon and I won't be able to afford to drive a new van. So I don't really know what to do."

"Have you tried to apply any models?"

"Well, I couldn't really think of anything special to do that might help. All I did was to list the alternatives, and the advantages and disadvantages for each alternative, but that seemed to miss the point. My choice depends on something that I have no control over—the price of gas. That seems to complicate the matter terribly."

Professor Gordian nodded. "I think that I have a model that might be helpful in a situation such as yours. It's called a payoff matrix." He reached through the open window behind him and got a pad of paper that was lying on the desk. He pulled his pen from his pocket and started to sketch some notes. "You say that you're interested in only two types of cars, vans and compacts?"

"I had considered pickup style campers, but they seem somewhat less convenient than vans because you don't have easy access to the cargo area without getting out of the car. And since the other type of car that I would be interested in would be cars that get good gas mileage, I think that I could lump them together as compacts."

strategies "Good. That's the first step in applying the model I have in mind—to classify the various alternative *strategies* available to you or to simplify the alternatives by aggregating them somehow. The classifications of vans and compacts seem appropriate considering your specific problem. The next thing to do is to classify what *states of nature* could ensue. These are the relevant conditions over which you have virtually no control. Once again you have to simplify by aggregation, and here it seems clear that what you are concerned with is the two alternatives of gas prices being prohibitive and gas prices not being prohibitive. Right?"

"Right. I am not really concerned with what specific price gas reaches, but whether it would put me in the poor house or not."

"OK, we can now create the framework for a payoff matrix." Professor Gordian sketched the diagram shown in Figure 47. The rows correspond to the two alternative strategies available to Alex, either buying a van or a compact, and the columns correspond to the two states of nature, gas prices being prohibitive or not. "All we have to do now is to fill in how satisfying each of the possible combinations of strategy and state of nature would be. We refer to each such combination as our outcome. For example, the upper left hand corner of the diagram is the outcome of buying a van and gas prices being affordable. This would naturally be your most preferred outcome, since you would have the type of car that you really want and you could afford to drive it.

"In the lower left hand corner you have a compact and gas prices would be such that you could afford to drive a van. This would seem to be an unpleasant outcome for you, since you would not have the car that you really wanted, and you would probably be kicking yourself in the pants for not having gotten the van instead. Also unpleasant for you would be the upper right hand corner, where you have a van, but cannot afford to drive it. Better would be the lower right hand corner, where you have a compact and gas is expensive. At least then you could drive around in your compact. What you need to do now is to assign some measure of your state of satisfaction to each of the possible outcomes.

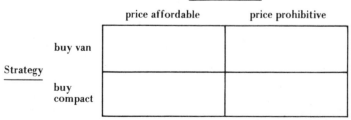

Figure 47. Skeleton of payoff matrix.

A number which is a measure of your state of satisfaction is called
utility a *utility*. There are many ways in which you could generate utilities. One of the simplest ways is just to rank order the outcomes.
You could assign a 'one' to the worst possible outcome, a 'two' to
the next worst outcome, and so on up until you have assigned a
'four' to the best outcome. If there were cases where you could
not decide between outcomes, you could assign the same ranking
to each outcome. You may assign identical rankings to a number
of outcomes if you wish. Why not go ahead and try that for this
payoff matrix?"

Alex took the paper from Professor Gordian and studied the
payoff matrix. "The worst outcome for me would be to have a van
and not be able to drive it, so I will assign a utility of one to that
outcome. The next worst outcome would be to have a compact
with high gas prices. I would not have the car I want and would be
paying a lot for gas, but at least I would be able to drive. Next
worst is having a compact with affordable gas prices. I would not
have the car that I want, but at least gas prices would be cheaper.
Best would be having a van with affordable gas prices."

Alex filled in the numbers (see Figure 48) from four to one and
handed the paper back to his uncle. "We now have a very useful
model for making decisions, Alex. Listed here are the possible
strategies for you, combined with the possible states of nature,
and your subjective assessment of satisfaction associated with each
outcome. Before we go on, I ought to point out that there are
more precise ways of assigning utilities, and for the purpose that
you have in mind we probably ought to use one of these more
sophisticated methods. In rank ordering the outcomes, you have a
list of best to worst outcomes, but you are ignoring the differences
between the adjacent rankings. For example, your best outcome is
having a van with affordable gas, and your second best outcome is

| | | State of Nature | |
		affordable	prohibitive
Strategy	buy van	4	1
	buy compact	3	2

Figure 48. Payoff matrix complete with rank ordered
utility.

having a compact with affordable gas, but these two outcomes might be miles apart in the way you feel about them."

"Well, there really is no comparison," interrupted Alex. "The car that I want is the van, and if I got the compact I would be unhappy with it."

"And," continued the professor, "your next best outcome is having a compact with high gas prices, and that outcome might be quite close to the outcome of having a compact with affordable gas. After all, the only difference is in how much you are paying for gas. You are saddled with your second choice car in both cases. The rankings do not reflect that the difference between your best and second best alternative is a lot greater than the difference between your second best and your third best. If you were to lay out your preferences along a line it might look like this." Professor Gordian sketched out the diagram in Figure 49.

"Yes, that's a pretty good picture of how I feel about the situation," commented Alex.

"In order for your utilities to reflect the size of the intervals between your ranked outcomes, you have to do more than just rank them. One way of coping with this problem is to pick some arbitrary interval, say from 0 to 10 or from 0 to 100, with the highest number representing the best conceivable outcome in the situation and the lowest number representing the worst possible outcome. It really does not matter what interval you choose. It could be from –10 to +10 or anything that is convenient, as long as you are consistent throughout your problem. This interval is now going to represent a subjective yardstick for measuring satisfaction. Say you had picked your interval to be from 0 to 10, then a value of five would represent relative indifference, that is, midway between the best conceivable outcome and the worst. Higher numbers represent a more favorable outcome and lower numbers represent a less desirable outcome. Assigning the same number to two different outcomes reflects indifference between them. The only restriction necessary in this scheme is that it forces your preferences to be *transitive*. That is, if you prefer one outcome to a second and the second to a third, then you must also

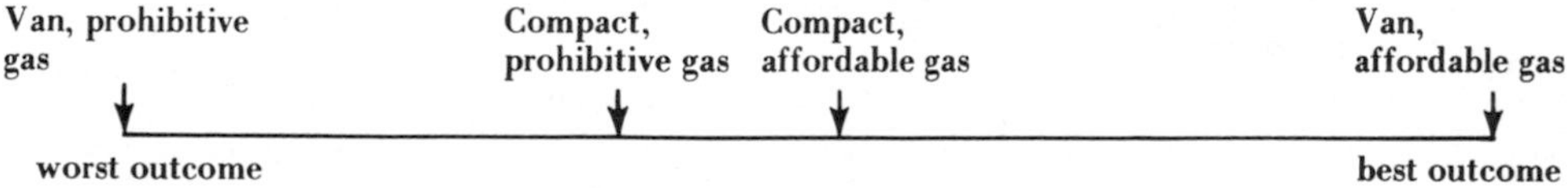

Figure 49. Professor Gordian's sketch of Alex's possible preferences.

prefer the first outcome to the third. This would have to be so or else you couldn't assign numbers to your outcomes and have the results make sense. For example, if you assigned a utility of ten to your best outcome and a utility of seven to your second, then to reflect that your second outcome was preferred to your third, the utility for the third outcome would have to be less than seven. So your first outcome with a utility of ten would still be preferred to the third outcome. This idea of transitivity is rational and makes sense. Yet it seems to be violated sometimes. For instance, you might walk into an ice cream store and the first thing that comes into your mind is that you want a strawberry ice cream cone. But wait, you say, you would rather have chocolate. And on third thought, you might prefer vanilla to chocolate. Upon thinking about that for a second or two, you might think that you would prefer strawberry to vanilla. You had better not try to assign utilities under such circumstances! To assign utilities you would have to settle down and decide at that time exactly what was your order of preferences. Not to do so would engage you in an endless circle: strawberry, chocolate, vanilla, strawberry, chocolate, vanilla, and so on until you died of starvation."

Alex nodded his understanding and Professor Gordian continued. "The main idea is that your preferences must be reflected in the numbers, with higher numbers representing more desirable outcomes, and the differences in preference must be reflected in the differences in the numbers. Would you like to try to assign utilities by this method to the outcomes in your payoff matrix?"

Alex picked up the paper and pondered for a moment. "I'll use the numbers from 0 to 10 for my scale, and since the best conceivable outcome is having a van with affordable gas prices, I will assign a utility of ten to that outcome. The next most favorable outcome is having a compact with affordable prices, and that represents a point of, well, relative indifference. I would have a new car at any rate. So I will assign a utility of five to that outcome. Next best would be having a compact with prohibitive gas prices, and that would be fairly unpleasant, so say a utility of three. And worst would be to have a van with prohibitive prices, so that is a utility of zero. Is that all there is to it?" Alex's matrix is shown in Figure 50.

"Yes, Alex, that is all there is to it. You now have a very useful model for making decisions. This type of model is appropriate for decision making whenever decisions are attendant upon some relevant states of nature over which we have no control. For example,

State of Nature

		affordable	prohibitive
Strategy	Van	10	0
	Compact	5	3

Figure 50. Payoff matrix with scaled utility.

a person might be interested in which of a number of investments to make, when the possible outcomes depend on the possible states of the economy. Or a farmer might be interested in what crop to plant when the yield would depend on weather conditions. It could even be used to represent the case of where a jury has to decide whether to convict or acquit a person who could be either innocent or guilty. Given that you can construct a payoff matrix, there are many rational, or at least systematic, ways for making a decision depending on the circumstances. To start out with, suppose that you knew for certain what would be the ensuing state of nature. How would you decide then?"

"That would be easy. Just look at the column corresponding to the state of nature that would occur, and pick the strategy with the highest utility. There would be no problem at all! If gas was sure to be affordable, I would choose a van because ten is greater than five, and if gas was to be prohibitive I would choose a compact because three is greater than zero."

"Right. Just for the record though, I should mention that under these circumstances, called 'decision under certainty,' things are not always so simple. In other situations where there are more than just two different strategies, the decision process can be more difficult. Suppose you had a situation with several thousand possible strategies, which in fact sometimes occurs. It might take a computer to efficiently determine which is the best strategy. Usually, however, for there to be a difficult problem, we need to be in a state of some uncertainty about what state of nature will ensue. Sometimes, though, we do know what the objective probabilities of the states of nature are. This is called 'decision under risk.' Suppose, for example, that you had consulted several economic experts and had determined that the probability of gas reaching prohibitive prices within the next five years would be 0.2. That would then mean that the probability of prices not reaching prohibitive levels would be 0.8. You are now in a position to make a rational

decision under certainty

decision under risk

139

decision based on a very reasonable criterion. That criterion is to *maximize your expected value of utility*. As you recall from our previous conversations, the expected value is the amount you would expect to win or lose on the average, and it can be computed by summing the product of the probabilities of outcomes times the values of those outcomes. If this was done with utilities, it would give you the average utility you might expect to achieve in the long run for any given decision. Why not try to calculate these values for your problem?"

Alex produced the table and details of Figure 51, then explained what he would do. "OK. To calculate the expected utility for a van, I multiply the probability of gas being affordable times the utility for that outcome and add to this the probability of gas being prohibitively priced times the utility for that outcome. That gives me 0.8 times ten plus 0.2 times zero which equals 8. Doing the same thing for compacts, I get 0.8 times five plus 0.2 times three which equals 4.6. So I would expect to do better by choosing the van!"

$$E[U \text{ (van)}] \quad = 0.8 \,(10) + 0.2 \,(0) = 8$$

$$E[U \text{ (compact)}] \quad = 0.8 \,(5) + 0.2 \,(3) = 4.6$$

"That's correct. But remember that you will *not* receive an outcome with a utility value of eight by getting the van. If you could hypothetically repeat the present situation time after time, you would *average* eight units of utility (called utiles). On any given try you would receive either ten 'utiles' or zero 'utiles.' You would expect to get 10 'utiles' 8/10 of the time and zero 'utiles' 2/10 of

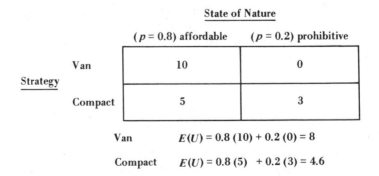

		State of Nature	
		($p = 0.8$) affordable	($p = 0.2$) prohibitive
	Van	10	0
Strategy			
	Compact	5	3

Van $\qquad E(U) = 0.8\,(10) + 0.2\,(0) = 8$

Compact $\qquad E(U) = 0.8\,(5) \;\; + 0.2\,(3) = 4.6$

Figure 51. Expected value solution.

the time. This is, of course, a strange conceptualization, since you cannot repeat the present situation! But you can think of it as taking the best bet. Would you rather bet on heads for the flip of a fair coin, or for a coin biased for heads? Naturally your expected value for the biased coin is better. And so it is here. You bet on the highest expected value, and pick the van. The maximum expected utility is used as a criterion for making a choice. But you will never actually realize this maximum expected utility in any single decision situation, no more than you would observe a single family with 2.672 children if this were the average number of children per family in a population.

"Remember also that the figures that I gave you for the probabilities of gas prices were just idle speculation. In order to use this strategy you have to be serious about determining reasonably accurate probabilities for the states of nature. If you could not come up with probabilities for the states of nature then you would have a situation known as '*decision under uncertainty*.' To make a decision under these circumstances you have to appeal to your inner emotional and judgmental states to tell you what to do. But you can be systematic in applying your criterion. decision under uncertainty

"There are several possible criteria available when attempting to make a decision under uncertainty. One such criterion is called the *subjectivist criterion*. A subjectivist may assign any subjective probability that he wishes to reflect his degree of knowledge or belief. As a subjectivist you may admit to yourself that you know nothing about which state of nature will ensue. By making that admission, you can assign probabilities to the states of nature on the basis of the principle of maximum uncertainty that we discussed in the past. With two alternative states of nature as in this example, you would assign probabilities of 1/2 to each to denote that you have no reason to expect that one would be any more likely than another. With more available states of nature, for instance three, you would divide the total probability of one into as many equal parts as there are states, in this case 1/3 apiece. After you have done this, you could then go ahead and maximize your expected outcome of utility. Would you like to try this?" subjectivist criterion

"Sure. It will be interesting to see how this one comes out compared with the other strategy that I just tried. Let's see, I'll take 1/2 times ten, plus 1/2 times zero, and get a sum of five for the van. For the compact I'll take 1/2 times five, plus 1/2 times three, and get four. So I reach the same decision!" The payoff matrix is shown in Figure 52.

State of Nature

affordable ($p = 1/2$)   prohibitive ($p = 1/2$)

	affordable ($p = 1/2$)	prohibitive ($p = 1/2$)
Van	10	0
Compact	5	3

Strategy

Van $E(U) = 1/2(10) + 1/2(0) = 5$

Compact $E(U) = 1/2(5) + 1/2(3) = 4$

Figure 52. Subjectivist criterion.

$$E[U \text{ (van)}] \quad = \frac{1}{2}(10) + \frac{1}{2}(0) = 5$$

$$E[U \text{ (compact)}] \quad = \frac{1}{2}(5) + \frac{1}{2}(3) = 4$$

"I can see that this is starting to reinforce your confidence in your choice of the van. There are still other criteria that are possible and reflect different attitudes of decision makers. One of these is called the *pessimist criterion*. The pessimist is a person who feels that whatever he does, things will go sour. This type has the frequent experience of going out on a sunny day, naturally without an umbrella, and getting wet in sudden rain. If he prepares for the worst and takes an umbrella, then it is invariably sunny and people give him strange looks for carrying around an umbrella on such an obviously nice day. This type of person can also usually get it to rain by washing the car or by watering the lawn. Poor people. You get the picture, the mythical 'born losers.' This type of person can avert risk in a decision process by determining what is the worst thing that can happen for each strategy, and then choosing the strategy that gives the best outcome in this worst of all possible worlds. For example, looking at your problem, if you were to get a van, the worst thing that could happen is that gas prices would become prohibitive, and you would receive zero 'utiles.' You can denote this by creating an additional third column next to the other two and labeling it 'row minima.'" This matrix is shown in Figure 53. "This is the worst possible outcome for each strategy. For a compact, the worst thing that could happen would once again be for gas prices to be prohibitive, in which case you

pessimist criterion

142

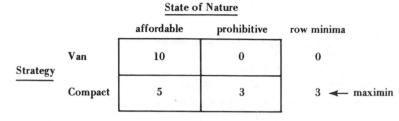

State of Nature

		affordable	prohibitive	row minima
Strategy	Van	10	0	0
	Compact	5	3	3 ← maximin

Figure 53. Pessimist criterion.

would be receiving three 'utiles.' The pessimist could then look at these row minima and choose the strategy that gives him the best of these. In this case, that would be to get a compact. This is called the *maximin criterion,* since you are choosing the best of the worst outcomes. If you did this, you could guarantee yourself that the worst thing that could happen to you would be to achieve only three 'utiles.' Notice how this differs from the expected utility criteria in which you could get unlucky after choosing the van, and gas prices could soar. It is this unlikely turn of events that the pessimist criterion is designed to protect you against."

"Well, any confidence that I was building up for getting a van just got quickly shattered. But you know, that pessimist attitude is a pretty grim thing. I understand how it averts risk and all, but no one could be such a complete pessimist in all situations that they would look only at the worst thing that could possibly happen. Isn't there a brighter attitude?"

"Yes there is, Alex. In fact there is a complete antithesis of the pessimist. That is the optimist. Have you ever noticed people that go around smiling all the time? People who have an air of invincible confidence? These are the optimists, the people who expect every-thing to turn out for the best. A person like this probably has a history of everything turning to gold beneath their touch or at least remembers only that part of the history. This type of person probably invested in Deutsche marks on a whim just before the devaluation of the dollar. A person like this could probably insure himself of indefinite sunshine by washing the car often enough. When faced with a decision like yours, an optimist would look at each available strategy and pick out the best possible outcome that could occur. To do this, you could make a new third column and label it *'row maxima'* to indicate the value for the best outcome for each strategy. An optimist would then pick the best of the best possible outcomes. This is called the *maximax criterion."*

maximin criterion

optimist criterion

maximax criterion

143

Alex chuckled. "This is starting to sound like a television commercial for laundry soap or something. Maximin, maximax, what comes next?"

Professor Gordian chuckled along with Alex. "Most workers in the fields in which these tools were developed are noted for their odd sense of humor. But I don't think that these terms were meant to be funny. It just turned out that way. What would you do with an optimist criterion Alex?"

Alex drew in the third column and labeled it *"row maxima"* as shown in Figure 54. He filled in a 10 in the van row and a 5 in the compact row. "Since 10 is the largest number in this column, it is the maximax and so I would choose the van. But seriously, this criterion seems as single minded as the pessimist criterion. This one looks only at the best outcomes, and if the pessimist strategy averts risk, then this one seems to seek risk. If I choose the van I could be unlucky, gas prices could soar, and then I would be in a fine fix. This strategy may appeal to some, but I am just not that much of an optimist. Is there some other criterion or attitude, maybe one in between these two extremes of optimism and pessimism?"

"It is interesting that you should state your question as you did, Alex, because there is such a criterion and it is known as an *inbetweenist criterion*. While the optimist looks only at the best outcomes and the pessimist looks only at the worst outcomes, the inbetweenist looks at both the best and the worst outcomes for each strategy. It tempers one with the other, so to speak. Before you can use this criterion you must decide to what degree you are an optimist or a pessimist, so as to know what relative weights to put on the best and worst outcomes. You can simply choose what you feel to be your relative proportion of optimism and pessimism. For example, if you are feeling neither optimistic nor pessimistic, you could say that you were 50 percent optimist and 50 percent pessimist. Or if you were moderately optimistic, you could say

inbetweenist criterion

	State of Nature		
	affordable	prohibitive	row maxima
Van	10	0	10 ◄— maximax
Compact	5	3	5

Strategy

Figure 54. Optimist criterion.

144

that you were 75 percent optimist and 25 percent pessimist. Let's say that you are 75 percent optimist. Then if you look at each strategy and devote 75 percent of your consideration to the best outcome and 25 percent of your consideration to the worst outcome, you are employing parts of both optimist and pessimist strategies. You could do this by taking 75 percent of the utility of the best outcome and adding 25 percent of the utility of the worst outcome. You would be weighing the best outcome more than the worst, and this would reflect your moderate optimism. You would then choose the strategy that had the highest sum of these weighted utilities. Would you like to try this strategy?"

"Sure! That sounds much more reasonable. Let's see. I'm an optimist, but not a real Pangloss. I would say that I am 60 percent optimist and 40 percent pessimist. For the van, if I take 60 percent of ten, which is the utility of the best outcome of gas being affordable, and add 40 percent of zero, which is the utility for the worst outcome, I get six. For the compact, I take 60 percent of five and 40 percent of three, and that is, let's see, 3 plus 1.2, or 4.2. Picking six, which is the larger of these two, I would decide to get the van. Of all the criteria for decision under uncertainty that you have shown me so far, this one makes the most sense." This matrix is shown in Figure 55.

$$E[U(\text{van})] = 0.60(10) + 0.40(0) = 6$$
$$E[U(\text{compact})] = 0.60(5) + 0.40(3) = 4.2$$

Alex stared vacantly into the air, smiling. "Hmmm. A van. That sure starts to sound good." But a frown quickly crossed his face. "You know, professor, that I just can't stop thinking about what

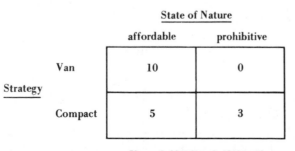

Van: $0.60(10) + 0.40(0) = 6$
Compact: $0.60(5) + 0.40(3) = 4.2$

Figure 55. Inbetweenist criterion.

would happen if I did get the van and gas prices soared and I couldn't drive it. Or for that matter, if I got a compact and gas prices remained within reason. I think that the latter would hurt just as much, because I would be stuck with a compact and I would really regret my not getting the van. This whole thing reminds me of when Dad sold his model T car just before the prices of those cars started soaring. If he had kept it just a few more months he could have gotten double what he had sold it for. I remember him cursing himself for days after that. Every morning he would stand at the window and look at the new car he bought with what he received for the old model T and moan at how expensive it had really been. It was even more expensive than he thought it was if he had only taken into account the amount of Rolaids that he consumed in the following year."

"Yes, I remember the anguish your father went through after that unfortunate decision. Missing an opportunity like that often leads to such terrible regret that some people would be willing to **regret** take any measure possible to insure against experiencing this kind **criterion** of pain. If this is an important factor to you, you can use decision theory to try to avoid regret. The process goes like this. You look at what would be the state of affairs, supposing you have made your decision and a given state of nature prevails. To be specific, suppose that you had decided to either get the van or the compact, which one does not matter for now, and gas prices had turned out to be affordable. You would look at the first column of your payoff matrix. If in fact you had decided to get the van, that would have been the best decision given the ensuing state of nature, and you would be experiencing no regret. But if you had decided to get the compact, you would only be getting five 'utiles' instead of the ten that you would have had with the van. You would then regret your decision. This regret could be measured by the difference between the utility for the best decision and the decision that you made, that is, the difference between ten and five, which amounts to five 'utiles.' You could enter these quantities into a **regret matrix** *regret matrix.*"

Professor Gordian sketched the diagram in Figure 56 and filled in the first column. "If after you had made your decision, gas prices had become prohibitive, then you would look at the second column of your payoff matrix. The best thing to have done here would have been to select the compact, after which there would have been no regret. But if you had selected the van, you would experience regret to the extent of the difference between the best

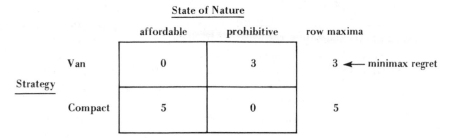

Figure 56. Regret matrix and regret criterion.

outcome and the outcome that you received, or three minus zero which is 3 'utiles.'"

Professor Gordian completed the regret matrix shown in Figure 56. "If you look at this regret matrix, you can see that it is a model of how much regret you would experience after you have made your decision for each of the two possible ensuing states of nature. If your aim is to avoid regret, you could employ a pessimist attitude to minimize the risk of regret. If you look at the first row (van) of the regret matrix, the worst thing that could happen is that gas prices would become prohibitive and you would consequently experience three 'utiles' of regret. If you had opted for the compact the worst thing that could have happened would be that gas remained affordable and you would experience five 'utiles' of regret."

Professor Gordian made a third column in the regret matrix of Figure 56 and labeled it "row maxima." "Notice that the worst possible thing that can happen is to have high regret, which is represented by the row maxima. This differs from the pessimist strategy where the matrix entries are utilities received. There the worst possibility would be for the numbers to be small, which would be the row minima." He filled in the third column to indicate the worst possible outcome for each strategy. "Since you now have a column of the worst possible things that could happen, you want to pick the best outcome from among these. That would be the smallest regret, or the 'three' associated with the first row. So if you chose the van you would be assured that the worst thing that could happen would be that you would experience three 'utiles' of regret."

Alex looked over the regret matrix and a smile spread over his face. "Very clever! You decision experts can even quantify regret. So I guess that even if I'm not able to invent a better mousetrap, I could determine how much I regret not being able to do so!"

"Quite true, but that would be a simple matter of just tuning into your own feelings and judgments. The models require you to first tune into your feelings and judgments in order to assign utilities, and then give you a logical framework for selecting among the possibilities. So tell me, what do you think about your decision now? Do you think that a van or a compact would be the best for you?"

"From what I have done so far, the van looks the most promising. The inbetweenist criterion suggests it, as does the regretist criterion. But I suppose that I should really try to obtain more information on the probabilities of the two relevant states of nature. That would allow me to make a more informed decision."

"Yes, indeed. It is always important to gather as much relevant and credible information as possible before finalizing a decision."

Once again Alex smiled sheepishly, and averting his gaze, addressed the professor. "Well, I have to admit that I have been doing a lot of daydreaming lately. What I really want is the van, in spite of my worries. I have been spending a lot of time trying to decide upon the best van, just in case I would eventually decide that the best choice is a van. And, not surprisingly, I have wound up with still another problem! Of three makes of van that I am considering, I cannot decide which one would be the best. Do you think that you could help me with this problem, too? I sort of feel like I am imposing since you are always helping me with my problems."

"Nonsense, Alex! You know better than that. What are uncles for, anyway? So you cannot decide which van to choose. What is bothering you about the decision?"

"It would be an easy decision if one type of van had all of the things that were desirable to me, but that just isn't the way things are. I like most of the features of one van the best, except that it is more expensive, and unfortunately will also be the most costly to operate since it gets the poorest fuel economy. The van which is the cheapest and which also gets the best fuel economy I don't like nearly as well. The metal is thin, the interior colors are gaudy, it rattles, and the overall workmanship is poor. The third alternative is just about intermediate in initial price and fuel economy, and I like its features about halfway between the first two makes, but I have read that the mechanical reliability is not too good. So I am in a quandary. What is the most important aspect in making the decision? I can't seem to adequately weigh the different alternatives on all of the relevant attributes, and then somehow synthesize the results into a meaningful whole. Do you have any suggestions?"

"This is a type of problem that is very common in decision multiattribute making, and it is called the *multiattribute decision problem*. It decision arises when there are several alternatives to choose among, but there are many relevant attributes in the decision and no alternative has any clearcut advantage on all of the attributes. This is a very common type of problem. Students cannot decide which major to pick, or what career to pursue. A person might not be able to decide on which of several houses to buy, or which of several jobs to take, or which of several calculators to buy. These problems arise constantly. What people tend to do in situations like this is to focus on only a very few attributes and neglect the others. In fact, in most instances people look only at one attribute and make slight corrections with only one other attribute. When contradictions arise, the second attribute is ignored and the decision is made solely on the basis of one attribute. I recall a study that was done with radiologists. The radiologists had determined beforehand that there were six different attributes important in deciding whether a tumor was malignant or not. When they were asked to diagnose a set of radiograms, they essentially used only one attribute, with small corrections for a second. This seems to be an inefficient method for making decisions, but it is what people do when there is too much information present to process at once. Remember that the number of unrelated items that a person can process in his short term memory at one time is seven plus or minus two, so attempting to choose between two alternatives on the basis of six attributes overwhelms the information processing capacity of the individual. There are ways of dealing with this problem, though, that seem somewhat more efficient in terms of utilizing all of the relevant information. Naturally, writing things down is helpful in any case where there is a stress on the memory. list attributes So you could first *list all the important attributes*. And since all of these attributes are probably not equally important, you could assign a weight to each in order to reflect its relative importance to you. If I were choosing a new car, both interior color and mechanical reliability would be important, but not nearly to the same degree. Can you think of any way that you are familiar with to assign weights to the attributes?"

"Sure! You showed me how to do that quite a while ago. That's relevance tree the relevance tree, right?"

"Right. Remember that the relevance tree is mainly useful when there are so many attributes that you cannot assign weights just by looking at the list. This occurs when the number of attributes is near to or exceeds the limit of the short term memory capacity of seven plus or minus two unrelated items. In order to assign accurate weights under these circumstances it is necessary to reduce the number of attributes that are dealt with at one time by arranging them in hierarchical fashion and then assigning weights within each level of the tree. If this is done properly then the number of items at each level of the tree will usually be well within the short term memory span. Have you thought much about all of the attributes that are important to you?"

With a look that almost said "Pshaw" Alex pulled a piece of paper out of his pocket. "Yes, I have been making a list over the past several days. I have not yet gotten down to assigning weights, though."

Alex handed the paper to Professor Gordian who looked it over carefully. Alex had listed the following attributes: exterior (trim, paint); interior; body integrity (rattles, squeaks, overall workmanship); initial cost; fuel economy; mechanical reliability; comfort; ride; handling and steering; brakes; warranty; and available options.

"Alright, Alex, so is this a list of all the attributes that are important to you?"

"These are all that I could think of so far."

"Can you eliminate any of the items from this list because they do not discriminate among your viable alternatives? Sometimes you can simplify your list of attributes because a few might not be relevant in deciding between alternatives. For example, you might be able to determine beforehand that all the alternatives are the same with respect to a given attribute. To illustrate, you would not include something like 'number of wheels' because the alternative cars do not differ on this attribute. Or more relevant, you would not include 'cargo capacity' if the vans did not differ significantly in this respect."

"That's a good point." Alex thought over the matter for a while and replied. "There are a couple of things that I could eliminate. These are warranty and available options. All three makes of car that I am considering have virtually the same type of warranty, and as far as I am concerned, the options do not differ. The list of available options differs, but not the options that I would choose. So I will just cross out these attributes as being irrelevant."

"As you recall, in the next step you must arrange the attributes in a hierarchy, since your ten attributes seem to be too many to accurately assign them weights without a relevance tree."

Alex surveyed his list of attributes and arranged them deliber-ately. "I think that the attributes fall naturally into four main categories; body, cost, reliability, and performance. Under body I would include interior, exterior, and workmanship. Under cost I would include initial cost and gas economy. I wouldn't further break down reliability. Under performance I would include handling and steering, brakes, ride, and comfort." As he spoke, Alex sketched out the relevance tree given in Figure 57. "Now I need to assign some weights. For the first level of the tree, I value reliability the greatest, followed by performance and cost which are about equal. Body is least important to me in a car. I think the weights of 1/8 for body, 1/4 for cost, 3/8 for reliability, and 1/4 for performance accurately reflect my feelings, as reliabil-ity seems to me to be about three times as important as body, and cost and performance are each about twice as important as body. Just to check. . . . yes, the sum of these weights is equal to one as it must always be in a relevance tree. Moving down to the second level of the tree, under body, I value interior and exterior about equally and each about half as much as workmanship, so I will assign weights of 1/4, 1/4, and 1/2, respectively. And under per-formance, handling and steering and brakes seem to be the most important, and each about twice as important as ride or comfort, so I will assign values of 1/3, 1/3, 1/6, and 1/6, respectively." Alex quickly wrote in these values, and then stopped to check his figures to make sure that the sum of the ·weights under each node equaled

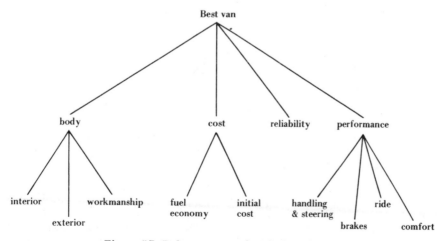

Figure 57. Relevance tree for choice of van.

one. "Now to multiply down the tree to obtain total weights for each attribute. I'll start on the left. Since interior contributes to 1/4 of my consideration of body, and since body contributes to 1/8 of my consideration of the whole van, then interior must be 1/4 of 1/8, or 1/32 of my consideration of the total van. For exterior I have 1/4 times 1/8, or 1/32 again, and for workmanship I have 1/2 times 1/8, or 1/16." Alex continued on and penciled in the products for each attribute, and then checked his arithmetic by making sure that the sum of all the final weights of all the attributes added to one. The final tree is shown in Figure 58. By breaking up the total list of attributes in a hierarchical fashion and assigning weights within each level of the tree, Alex was able to overcome the limitations on his information processing capacity. It is easy to assign weights to three or four attributes, but not to ten or more. Multiplying down the tree then allows reconstitution of the separate judgments into one coherent whole. The result is the assignment of logically consistent weighting factors to a greater number of attributes than could be readily done without the relevance tree.

"Well done, Alex. These weighting factors will be important to you in the next step of the decision model that I will describe. You can now construct another kind of model in which you rate each of your alternatives on each of the attributes that you have listed as relevant. I suggest a diagram like this."

Professor Gordian took the paper from Alex and sketched the

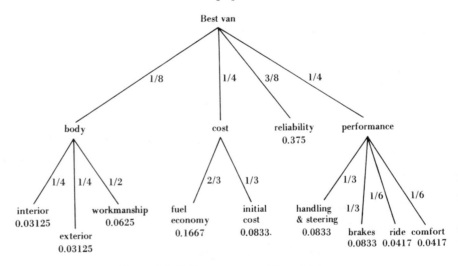

Figure 58. Relevance tree with weights.

table shown in Figure 59. Down the left column was a list of all the attributes and in the adjacent column immediately to the right were the weighting factors that Alex had just generated. Then came three separate wide columns labeled Alternatives *A, B,* and *C,* one for each van.

"The next step is to go through your list of attributes for each alternative and, where possible, fill in some objective value for future reference. For example, you probably do not have any objective or readily quantifiable data to evaluate interior, exterior, or workmanship in the different vans, but you could fill in a value for fuel economy in mpg, and you could also fill in a dollar value for initial cost. If you are familiar with it, there is a consumer publication which publishes a reliability index for various cars that you could fill in for your reliability row. If there is not a readily available reference figure then leave the row blank or fill in an asterisk."

Alex went through and filled in initial cost, mpg, and reliability indices that he had remembered from his careful survey of recent articles on the vans. When he was finished the professor continued. "Now what really concerns you here is not the objective index values that you have just written down, but how *satisfying* each alternative is to you on each of the attributes. You also want to be able to get some summary value for each car on all of the attributes combined, so you need to convert the data you have to some measure of satisfaction."

attribute	weight	Alternative A			Alternative B			Alternative C		
	w	ϕ	v	wv	ϕ	v	wv	ϕ	v	wv
interior	0.03125	*	4	0.125	*	0	0	*	1	0.031
exterior	0.03125	*	3	0.094	*	0	0	*	2	0.062
workmanship	0.0625	*	2	0.125	*	0	0	*	0	0
fuel economy	0.1667	15 mpg	2	0.333	20 mpg	4	0.667	18 mpg	3	0.500
initial cost	0.0833	$4800	3	0.250	$4200	6	0.500	$4300	5	0.416
reliability	0.375	50%	5	1.875	50%	5	1.875	40%	4	1.500
handling & steering	0.0833	*	0	0	*	3	0.250	*	1	0.083
brakes	0.0833	*	4	0.333	*	5	0.416	*	4	0.333
ride	0.0417	*	0	0	*	1	0.042	*	4	0.167
comfort	0.0417	*	5	0.2085	*	3	0.125	*	5	0.208
Σ w = 1.00				3.344			3.875			3.302

Figure 59. Multiattribute decision matrix. In this figure ϕ is an objective measure on each attribute and v is utility.

"Like utility!" exclaimed Alex.

"Precisely. Now go through each alternative for each attribute and assign utility values. Remember to survey all possible values of each attribute to get your decision into the proper context. For example, for the interior, you should not only compare the interiors of the three alternatives that you are considering, but you should evaluate them against a hypothetical ideal interior. Thus the best available interior in your list of alternatives need not receive the highest possible utility, and the worst available interior need not receive the lowest possible utility. You might find that all of the interiors are unsatisfactory, with some being worse than others. Or alternatively, they all might be pleasing to you with some more so than others. The important thing is to be consistent in the application of your chosen scale within each attribute."

"Well, let's see. Since my judgments are necessarily fairly rough, I am going to adopt a coarse utility scale that ranges from 0 to 6, with 0 being worst and 6 being best. Three would be neutral. That way I have three degrees of favorable judgment and three degrees of unfavorable judgment. Is that alright?"

"Yes, it is. If you were able to make finer discriminations, you might choose a more extended range for your utilities. But in this instance, a range of seven seems adequate."

"OK. Now I'll consider the first attribute, interior. Make *B* has the worst imaginable interior, so I'll give it a utility of zero. Make *C* is not a whole lot better, so I'll give it a one. Make *A* is quite a bit better than the other two, but I can still imagine a much nicer interior. I guess none of them really turns me on. I'll give make *A* a four."

"So you find the interior of make *A* to be only slightly pleasing?"

"Yes, I would say that. To look at the exterior next, once again make *B* is horrible. Make *C* is better, but by no means good, and make *A* is slightly better than make *C*. I am still only neutral to make *A*, so I will assign a three to *A*, a zero to *B*, and a two to *C*. For workmanship, both *B* and *C* are abominable, and *A* is a little better, but still bad. I'll assign a zero to both *B* and *C* and a two to *A*."

Alex went through all of the attributes and assigned the utilities given in Figure 59. When he was through, Professor Gordian spoke. "You now have a nice model for making decisions, Alex. For each attribute important to you, you have assigned a utility. You might think that all you would have to do is to sum or average the utilities for each alternative, but you must be careful. If you just added up the column of utilities, you would be giving each attribute equal weight in your decision. But you have already determined that the attributes are not equally important, and you have in fact assigned relative weights to each of them. What you need to do is to find a *weighted* average of utilities for each alternative. You can obtain this by multiplying the utility for each attribute by its relative weight before adding."

Alex then went through the table and did the work shown in Figure 59. For each row he multiplied the weighting factor, w, by the utility, v, thus creating a new column, wv, for each alternative. When he was through with that he added up the new columns he had just created.

"Now does this tell me that I should choose make B because the weighted average utility is the highest?"

"Yes, the model indicates that you would be most satisfied with alternative B. An ideal alternative, the best in every attribute, would yield a weighted average utility of six. The worst would yield a value of zero. The value of 3.875 for B indicates a slightly favorable alternative. You can see that the nice thing about this model is that it allows you to take into account a lot more information than you would normally be able to assimilate. By analyzing the alternatives into simple attributes you can make several individual decisions and then combine these decisions back together to get a weighted average."

"This is a very clever system, but one thing worries me. The weighted averages are all so close together, I still don't have a lot of confidence that I would be doing the right thing by choosing van B."

"Naturally the weighted averages are close together, because you could not make a decision before using the model. If one of the alternatives was vastly superior to all the others, you would probably not have to use the model because a decision would be easy. Some people who attempt to use this model fear that it is unreliable, since if the weighted averages are so close together they think they might be able to completely change the decision by just a minor change in say, one utility. They don't feel secure about assigning extremely precise utilities. But the model is not as sensitive to very minor changes as they think. All you need to do is to consider that any change in utility will be multiplied by a usually small weighting factor before it is summed. This serves to minimize instability and increase reliability."

Alex looked down at his feet, lost in thought. When he looked up at Professor Gordian he still had a deeply furrowed brow. "What if I had been able to make a clear choice without the model, and then gone ahead and applied the model anyway just to see how it would come out? Would it have to indicate the choice that I had originally chosen?"

"It would, provided that you had been accurate in listing all important attributes to you and had accurately assigned weights and utilities. It is interesting that you bring this up, because it illustrates another useful aspect of this model. If you already decided that one alternative was the best, then the model might help you find out something about yourself. If the model does not indicate the same choice as you would have originally made, then you can go back and examine the utilities and weighting factors that you have assigned and try to make the model work out. In this way you might discover something about your values. For instance, if you had been dissatisfied with the choice of van *B*, which the model indicated would be best, it might be because you had perhaps valued fuel economy too much or the appearance factors too little. Or perhaps you were taking into account some inappropriate context when you assigned a utility. It could also be because you had left out some important attribute. For instance, if there are more make *B* vans on the road than any other, and you value being different, then you might not want to choose *B*. Or perhaps an acquaintance of yours that you do not like has a van of make *B*. Going back through the model and searching for reasons might help you understand yourself better.

"Incidentally, speaking of understanding yourself better, there is another application of this model that is similar to a sophisticated version of the use of that universal mystical prognosticator, the coin. I am not speaking of using the coin to make your decision for you and then sticking by it, but a more refined version of the same game. You assign one alternative to heads and the other to tails, and then flip the coin and observe the outcome. Carefully try to observe your emotions when you see the fall of the coin. If you are elated, then the choice indicated by the coin is probably not bad, at least in terms of the way you feel at the present moment. But if you are disappointed, then you probably subconsciously wanted the other alternative, and could plan your choice accordingly. This is not to say that raw emotions should govern all choices, or even a substantial proportion of them, but sometimes you do not even know how you feel. The coin trick can help you find out. The same is true of the multiattribute decision model. You could work through the model and see if you are disappointed with the choice that it indicates. The advantage of using the model is that it allows you to go back and try to find out why you are dissatisfied. It gives you a more systematic method of contributing to your self-knowledge than does the coin trick."

Alex was smiling through all of this. "I have often used a coin to make seemingly impossible decisions, but I have never used it to help me discover my subconscious feelings. The possibility of using the decision model to do the same thing seems really useful. Many times I will make a decision on the basis of some factor that I am not really aware of, only to regret my decision later. The model might help me to discover what criterion I was really using to make my decision. I could avoid some really bad decisions that way. I remember a few years ago when I bought a racing bicycle. I later discovered that I had chosen the wrong type of bicycle for my purposes. The bike that I had gotten was so stiff that it jarred my fillings loose on every little bump in the pavement. The seat was uncomfortable, and it had the wrong kind of tires so that I was constantly fixing flats. I would have been much better off with a cheaper model that was more practical for my purposes. After I had thought about it for a long time I discovered that the reason that I wanted that bicycle was because I was really fascinated with bike racing and I was harboring a secret fantasy that I might be able to get into it as a competitor. All the time, though, I realized that I would never have the time to train adequately. I was also taken by the image of myself on such a 'neat' bike. But I was silly to spend so much money on something that was not appropriate. If I had made a decision model, even though I was pretty sure which bicycle I had wanted, I might have had some second thoughts. I might have discovered why it was that I wanted the racing bike, and perhaps might have even controlled myself."

So decision models are not a substitute for thinking, they are tools for thinking. They help us identify what matters, what is important to us, what we can and cannot control, and in the process they serve as an inner mirror to teach us some things about ourselves.

Later that evening Alex summarized the things he had learned that day in his intellectual diary.

SUMMARY

1/ The payoff matrix is a useful decision making model when the outcomes of a decision depend on something over which the decision maker has no control. The payoff matrix includes three elements: strategies or courses of action open to the decision maker, states of nature or that factor over which the decision maker has no control, and the outcomes associated with each combination of strategy and state of nature.

2/ The outcomes in a payoff matrix can be evaluated with utilities. A utility is a subjective measure of state of satisfaction and can be measured in two ways. Outcomes can be rank ordered from worst to best and the resulting ranks can serve as utilities, or some arbitrary scale can be adopted in which the numbers represent a continuum of satisfaction from a hypothetical best possible outcome to a hypothetical worst possible outcome. Utilities are then assigned as numbers on a scale which represents the corresponding degree of satisfaction associated with each actual outcome. The latter method is more sensitive and reflects the relative spacing of the outcomes.

3/ Decision under certainty refers to the situation where the decision maker is certain as to which state of nature is to ensue. He then merely has to pick the strategy with the highest available utility for that given state of nature.

4/ Decision under risk refers to the situation where the decision maker knows the probabilities of the possible states of nature. He should select the strategy with the highest expected value of utility. This is the strategy that would give the maximum amount of satisfaction in the long run, and is therefore the best bet.

5/ Decision under uncertainty refers to the situation where not even the probabilities of the states of nature are known. There are then at least five different criteria that can be used to make a decision:

a/ subjectivist criterion: the decision maker assigns subjective probabilities to the states of nature in accordance with his personal assessment. He then uses a maximum expected value criterion to choose among strategies.

b/ pessimist criterion: the decision maker finds the worst possible outcome for each strategy and picks the strategy with the best of these worst possible outcomes. This maximin criterion minimizes risk by assuring that the actual outcome can be no worse than a given value.

c/ optimist criterion: The decision maker finds the best possible outcome for each strategy and then picks the strategy with the best of these best possible outcomes. This maximax criterion seeks risk by not taking into account what is the worst possible outcome that could occur.

d/ inbetweenist criterion: the decision maker finds a weighted average between the best possible outcome and the worst possible outcome for each strategy. The weighting factors represent the decision maker's balance of optimism and pessimism.

e/ regretist criterion: the decision maker minimizes the risk of regret by using a pessimist criterion on a regret matrix. The regret matrix is generated by finding the best possible outcome for each state of nature and then finding the difference between that outcome and the rest of the outcomes for each state of nature. This difference represents the regret associated with each combination of state of nature and strategy. The decision maker then finds the maximum regret possible with each strategy, and picks the strategy with the smallest maximum regret.

6/ A relevance tree is a way of assigning weights to the different attributes which make up some alternative. The first step is to list all of the attributes making up some alternative and then arrange them in a hierarchy in a tree, with the subordinate or component attributes below each major attribute. Starting at the top of the tree, the decision maker assigns weights to the branches below each node in a way that reflects the relative importance of the attributes. The weights below each node sum to one. Then the decision maker multiplies the weights down the tree to determine the overall weight for each component attribute.

7/ In a multiattribute decision problem where you must decide upon the best of several alternatives, each with many different attributes, first construct a relevance tree to assign weights to the common attributes. Then list these attributes in the leftmost column of a multiattribute decision matrix. In the next column list the weights for the attributes. Next list the different alternatives to the right, with three separate columns for each alternative. In the first column for each alternative, assign some objective value, if available, for each attribute. In the second column for each alternative, assign a utility for each attribute. In the third column for each alternative multiply the utilities and weights together to yield a product for each attribute. Finally, sum these products for each alternative and choose the one with the highest weighted average utility.

8/ Decision models are not a substitute for thinking. They are tools for thinking, as are models in general.

PROBLEMS

1/ A farmer has to decide what crop to plant in a given area. Suppose that he has four strategies: to plant asparagus, peas, tomatoes, or do nothing. The states of nature can be summarized in four possiblities: perfect weather, good weather, variable weather, and bad weather. The utilities of the outcomes under these conditions are summarized in the payoff matrix below:

STATES OF NATURE

STRATEGIES	perfect	good	variable	bad
plant asparagus	12	5	4	0
plant peas	10	6	6	3
plant tomatoes	9	8	7	3
plant nothing	4	4	4	4

What strategy should be selected if the farmer uses:
a/ a subjectivist strategy (use your own subjective probability assignments)
b/ a pessimist criterion
c/ an optimist criterion
d/ an inbetweenist criterion (use your own balance between optimism and pessimism)
e/ a maximum expected value criterion given that he knows that the probabilities for perfect, good, variable, and bad weather are 0.1, 0.3, 0.4, and 0.2, respectively.

2/ It is Sunday night and you have to decide whether to study hard for your Monday morning class, just skim through the notes, or watch TV. You have no idea whether there will be a quiz the next day, and if there is whether it will be easy or difficult. What would your strategy be, given the following payoff matrix showing the utility of each outcome, for each of the following criteria:
a/ a subjectivist criterion (use your own subjective probability assessments)

b/ a pessimist criterion
c/ an optimist criterion
d/ an inbetweenist criterion (use your own balance between optimism and pessimism)
e/ a maximum expected value criterion given that you know from past experience that the probabilities of no quiz, an easy quiz, or a hard quiz are 0.4, 0.3, and 0.2, respectively.

	no quiz	easy quiz	difficult quiz
study hard	7	5	8
skim notes	6	8	7
watch TV	10	4	0

3/ Two doctors are trying to decide whether they should treat a certain patient or wait. Their respective utilities for the three outcomes: cure, death, and paralysis, are as follows:

	U(cure)	U(paralysis)	U(death)
Doctor 1	100	40	0
Doctor 2	100	0	−200

The probabilities of the three outcomes based on the action taken are as follows:

	Cure	Paralysis	Death
Treat	0.6	0.1	0.3
Wait	0.4	0.5	0.1

Given the above information (show all work):
a/ will Doctor 1 decide to treat or wait?
b/ will Doctor 2 decide to treat or wait?

4/ Given the following relevance tree for the purchase of a new car and the alternatives and utilities below, determine the best choice.

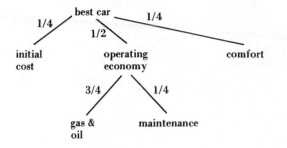

Figure 60. Relevance tree for Problem 4.

	initial cost	gas & oil	maintenance	comfort
Auto 1	20	24	96	80
Auto 2	36	72	8	56
Auto 3	76	56	48	12

PROJECT

Select a multiattribute decision type problem that you have and analyze it using the methods of this chapter. Construct a relevance tree and assign weights, then assign utilities to each attribute for each alternative. Good problems for this type of analysis are: what major to choose in school, what career goal to pursue, what to do next summer, what calculator (or watch, or camera, or stereo, etc.) to buy, whether to buy or rent a house, whether to fix up an old car or buy a new car or lease one, etc.

5

Decision Making
under Conflict

can anyone be trusted?

Alex was sitting at the edge of his seat listening to Professor Gordian lecture. There were about fifty students in the class ranging from undergraduates to graduate students. Alex observed with amazement that the dialogue style of his uncle's personal conversations also characterized his interaction with the class. It was evident from the questions and comments that the students had diverse backgrounds representing many fields of interest.

Professor Gordian placed a transparency on the overhead projector, and the matrix of Figure 61 was projected on the screen.

"Here is a model of a situation," said Professor Gordian, "in which two people, A and B, each have one choice out of two alternative actions. We label these *cooperate* and *defect* for reasons that will become apparent later. A and B are in the business of selling gasoline in different parts of the same town. From time to time there is a gasoline price 'war.' Experience has indicated to A

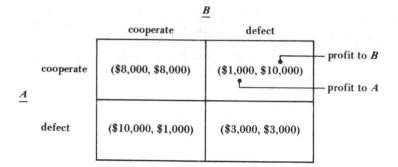

Figure 61. Profits to *A* and *B* for four consequences involving cooperation and defection. *A*'s profit is the left hand number in each outcome cell; *B*'s profit is the right hand number.

and *B* that it may be better to stop 'cutting each other's throat' with competition and reach an agreement to cooperate, on the basis of studying the model on the screen.

"*A* and *B* were students in our problem solving class," the Professor said jokingly, "and they appreciate the value of thinking with models. The first of the two numbers in each of the four cells, or outcomes, of the figure indicates the expected profit in thousands of dollars to *A* for a three month period. The second number represents expected profits to *B* for the same period. For example, if both *A* and *B* *cooperate* and abide by an agreement to keep a fixed price of gasoline, then they each can expect to realize a profit of $8,000 as shown in the upper left corner of the matrix. If they both *defect* and violate the agreement by lowering prices, then each will receive a $3,000 profit as seen in the lower right corner of the matrix. If *A* goes on a long vacation, for example, and leaves strict instructions to his assistants to abide by the agreement, and *B* defects by lowering his prices, then *B* will lure more customers to his station. By lowering his prices, *B* will realize a $10,000 profit, while *A*'s profit will be only $1,000. This is shown by the outcome in the upper right corner of the matrix. What is the situation in the lower left corner of the matrix?"

A student raised his hand and responded. "This is the outcome (defect, cooperate) in which *A* defects and *B* cooperates. It represents the case in which *B* abides by the agreement and *A* defects by lowering his prices. *A* lures more customers to his station and realizes a $10,000 profit because of the increase in volume of sales, despite his lower prices. *B* realizes only a $1,000 profit because very few customers will pay his higher price, and the higher price cannot offset the reduction in the number of customers."

"Very good" said Professor Gordian. "Now let us consider three specific attitudes that characterize human problem solvers in such a situation. Let us focus on *A* first.

There is a *temptation* for *A* to defect, given that *B* cooperates.

There is the *gain* from mutual cooperation as compared with mutual defection.

There is the *risk* that *A* may take by choosing to cooperate because *B* might betray him and defect.

temptation, gain, risk

Please take a few minutes to talk with each other and identify the monetary values associated with *temptation, gain,* and *risk* as *A* sees them in the matrix on the screen."

The class turned into a beehive, with everyone talking at once. When a hand went up in the middle of the room, Professor Gordian walked over to the student. Following a brief discussion, Professor Gordian returned to the front of the class and tapped the case of the overhead projector with a metal pointer. The talking subsided.

"Class," started the Professor, "John has an interesting observation to share with us. As you recall, in this class we sometimes start the discussion of a topic in the middle and let you discover and fill in the missing details in the beginning and the end. I once started reading a book on page 173, because I happened to open it there and was fascinated by what I saw. I continued reading to the end of the book and couldn't wait to return to the beginning to find out how it started. It was a most enjoyable experience."

John, the student who had talked to Professor Gordian earlier, made his way to the front of the room.

"Well," said John, "our group started talking about *temptation, gain,* and *risk* as *A* sees them, and the dilemma of cooperation versus defection that seems to depend so much on the uncertainty of mutual trust. We then decided to take a selfish attitude and consider what is best for *A*, regardless of what *B* might do. On that basis we concluded that *A* should always defect. Here is how we arrived at this conclusion: Suppose *B* cooperates, then *A* gets $8,000 if he cooperates and $10,000 if he defects. So *A* is better off defecting. Now suppose *B* defects, then *A* gets $1,000 if he cooperates and gets $3,000 if he defects. Again *A* is better off defecting.

"So regardless of what *B* does, *A* is better off defecting. If you inspect the first number, which is the payoff to *A*, in each outcome of the two rows in the matrix you see:

		B	
		cooperate	*defect*
A	*cooperate*	$ 8,000	$1,000
	defect	$10,000	$3,000

dominant strategy The profit from defect *dominates* the profit from cooperate for *A*. $10,000 is larger than $8,000 and $3,000 is larger than $1,000. *A* has a *dominant strategy* in *defect* because it is better than cooperate regardless of what *B* does."

"But wait a minute, John," interrupted another student. "It seems to me that a similar reasoning can be employed by *B* if he elects to look out for himself and be selfish as you have assumed *A* might do."

"Very good, Nancy," responded Professor Gordian. "Please come up here and take *B*'s position as you have suggested." John returned to his seat and Nancy came to the front of the class. Alex was impressed with the fact that Professor Gordian seemed to know the names of the students in this class of 50.

Nancy pointed to the first row of the matrix in Figure 61 and started talking. "Suppose *A* cooperates, then *B*, whose profits are represented by the second number on the right of each outcome, will receive $8,000 if he cooperates and $10,000 if he defects. So *B* is better off defecting when *A* cooperates. Now suppose *A* defects, then *B* gets $1,000 if he cooperates and $3,000 if he defects. Again he is better off defecting.

"So regardless of what *A* elects to do, *B* is better off defecting. In fact, to complete the analogy, if you inspect the second number, which is the payoff to *B* in each outcome of the two columns in the matrix, you see:

		B	
		cooperate	*defect*
A	*cooperate*	$8,000	$10,000
	defect	$1,000	$ 3,000

The profits from *defect* dominate the profits from *cooperate*.

$10,000 is larger than $8,000 and $3,000 is larger than $1,000. So *B* has a *dominant* strategy in defect because it is better than co-operate, regardless of what *A* does."

"So if we accept this mode of reasoning," a student called out, "*A* and *B* will both independently choose to defect and get $3,000 each, whereas mutual cooperation could have given each of them $8,000. Something must be wrong."

"Please take a few minutes to talk to each other about this last comment," suggested the Professor, "and please remember the words *temptation, gain,* and *risk* that I introduced earlier."

The class again turned into a mass of activity. The discussion was lively and exciting. After a while Professor Gordian tapped on the case of the overhead projector with the metal pointer, and the talking stopped.

"Well, class," he proceeded, "any comments on the dilemma facing *A* and *B* in our model? Can you detect a difference between *individual rationality* and *group rationality* as criteria for a choice of action?"

A student spoke up. "It seems to me that if we mean by *individual* rationality that one ought to look out for oneself and be selfish, then the present model suggests that *A* and *B* will each be better off when they are both irrational rather than rational, namely choosing to cooperate instead of defect. But the key feature is that both must choose to do so, and this of course requires mutual trust." **individual rationality**

"This is an interesting and perceptive observation, David," responded Professor Gordian. "The philosopher Immanuel Kant suggested a form of *collective rationality* that called for the following criterion as a guide for choice of action: *Act in such a way that if others also acted the same way you would benefit thereby.* This suggests an ethical principle of behavior involving mutual trust or a group rationality instead of an individual rationality. **collective rationality**

"Now before the end of the hour let us turn our attention to *temptation, gain* and *risk;* the "TiGeR," or TGR for short. Let us take *A*'s position; the symmetry of our model suggests that we can do the same for *B*. You can do that for homework.

"If *A* and *B* agree to cooperate, they will each receive $8,000. What *temptation* may enter *A*'s mind?"

Jean responded, "Given that *B* cooperates, *A* may be tempted to defect and thus get $10,000 instead of $8,000. So there is the *temptation* for the extra $2,000."

"Good. What is the *gain* from mutual cooperation as compared to mutual defection?" asked the Professor.

"The *gain* is the difference between \$8,000 and \$3,000, or a gain of \$5,000 for each," responded another student.

"Now we come to the question of *risk*. What amount will *A* risk if he elects to cooperate instead of defecting, and *B* defects?" asked the Professor.

A number of students spoke up together but the message was intelligible. Professor Gordian summarized. "Yes, you are right. If *B* defects, then *A* could have received \$3,000 by defecting. By electing to cooperate, *A* takes the *risk* of receiving only \$1,000, which is \$2,000 less."

Professor Gordian looked at his watch, then spoke, "Class, we have five minutes left. Let me give you some food for thought, and a reading assignment for next time." He placed a new transparency (shown in Figure 62) on the overhead projector.

"Row and Column are two nations, and the numbers represent billions of dollars gained. Positive numbers represent profit or saving and negative numbers represent loss or expenditure. For example, the outcome (arm, arm) leads each nation to spend five billion dollars. The outcome (arm, disarm) leads to Row taking over Column. Column then loses eleven billion dollars in goods and services to Row. But since Row continues to arm at a cost of five billion dollars, the net gain is 11 − 5 = 6 billion dollars. In the outcome (disarm, arm), Column takes over Row with analogous results.

"Please think about this model and identify the same features of *temptation, gain, risk,* trust, mistrust, and individual versus collective rationality.

"The next transparency shows a classical model known as the prisoner's dilemma." Actually the models of Figures 61 and 62 are also prisoner's dilemma models. Professor Gordian placed the transparency of Figure 63 on the projector. "Here the numbers represent years in prison for *A* and *B* depending on their choices of whether to *confess* or to *not confess.* You will find this model similar to those we discussed earlier today. Here *confess* corresponds to defecting in the gasoline price war, or to arm in the model for the two nations. The only difference is the fact that the objective here is to obtain fewer years in prison (i.e., a smaller payoff) rather than more profit or savings.

"For the next class meeting, please complete the reading of Chapter 7 on Decision Making Models in our course textbook. The material we discussed today is in the second half of the chapter. See you next time."

Column

	disarm	arm
disarm	(5, 5)	(-11, 6)
arm	(6, -11)	(-5, -5)

Row

Figure 62. Two nation payoff matrix (in billions of dollars.)

Prisoner B

	do not confess	confess
do not confess	(4, 4)	(12, 2)
confess	(2, 12)	(9, 9)

Prisoner A

Figure 63. Prisoner's dilemma payoff matrix.

As the students left the class, Alex walked up to Professor Gordian. Together they started toward the door.

*   *   *   *

Alex could not wait to try the prisoner's dilemma problem of Figure 63. He started by taking the position of prisoner *A* and reasoned aloud as he pointed to the numbers in the payoff matrix written in his notebook.

"Suppose *A* is looking out for himself. Then if *B* does not confess, *A* gets four years if he does not confess and only two years if he confesses. So *A* is better off confessing. If *B* confesses, *A* gets twelve years if he does not confess and only nine if he confesses. So again *A* is better off confessing." Alex looked up at Professor Gordian and concluded, "Regardless of what *B* does, *A* is better off confessing."

171

"What about *B*'s position?" asked the Professor.

Alex inspected the numbers and proceeded with his analysis. "Suppose *B* is looking out for himself. Then if *A* does not confess, *B* is better off confessing because then he gets only two years instead of the four that he would get if he were not to confess. And if *A* confesses, *B* is still better off confessing, because he gets nine years instead of the 12 he would get if he were not to confess. So regardless of what *A* does, *B* is better off confessing."

Alex looked up at the Professor and continued. "That's exactly what happened with the example in class today. If each one looks out for himself (confess), they each get nine years in prison. But if they cooperate (not confess) they each get four years in prison instead of nine."

"Yes, Alex, but what is the catch?"

"Mutual trust" answered Alex. "If one of them doesn't confess, the other may be tempted to confess and cut his term in prison from four to two years. And the one who chooses not to confess takes the risk of getting 12 years instead of nine if the other betrays him and confesses.

game theory   "It's amazing how much content was extracted from this model of four outcomes represented by the four pairs of numbers. Is this what *game theory* is all about?"

two-person   "This is one type of game theory model," said Professor Gordian.
nonzero-sum "It's called a *two-person nonzero-sum game.*" Professor Gordian
game pointed to the diagrams in Alex's notebook and indicated that the models of Figures 61, 62, and 63 have the general form of Figure

prisoner's 64, also known as a *prisoner's dilemma.* "In a prisoner's dilemma
dilemma model the preference ordering of outcomes for *A* and *B* is $a>b>c>d$. That is, *a* is the most preferred and *d* is the least preferred. Check the validity of this in these diagrams." Professor Gordian pointed to Figures 61, 62, and 63.

"In a prisoner's dilemma problem:

The *gain* from mutual cooperation compared to mutual detection is measured by $b - c$.

The *temptation* to defect when the other cooperates is measured by $a - b$.

The *risk* of cooperating when the other defects is measured by $c - d$.

"Here, Alex. If you are interested in this model of a problem

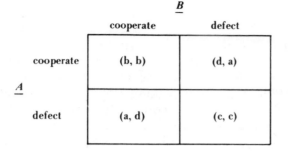

Figure 64. The general form of the prisoner's dilemma.

solving situation then read the material that I assigned to the class. You may use my copy of the book."

"Thanks. Can I keep it for a few days?" asked Alex.

"Sure thing!" replied Professor Gordian.

*   *   *   *

When Alex arrived at Professor Gordian's house Sunday, he found the Professor in the backyard reading the Sunday paper. "Did you hear the news this morning, Professor?" started Alex with excitement.

The Professor looked up with surprise: "What news?"

"A man is holding a hostage in a bank at gunpoint and the police are trying to convince him to surrender. It's been going on for a few hours now. It seems like a conflict between two sides, the gunman on the one hand and the law or society on the other. I thought the model you presented in class this week, or something similar to it, could help clarify the alternative actions and the outcomes in this situation. It appears that trust and mistrust and other elements of the model you presented are in evidence here between the two players, the gunman and the law. Surely there are mixed motives for each side in this situation."

"I'm glad, Alex, that you suggested the model as a tool for thinking and clarification and not for a conclusive solution, because models are representations that are prone to errors of omission and commission as well as inaccurate assessments of outcomes. We have to be very, very careful about where, when, and how to use them."

*   *   *   *

Alex spent the next two days studying the material Professor Gordian assigned his class. As he did so he thought of various conflict situations in which game theory models could be used as tools for thinking and decision making. He prepared a few pages of detailed notes in which he recorded the new concepts in the reading assignment. He first entitled his notes: Games People Play. However, when he completed the reading assignment he changed that to: Is that what you call a game? These notes are presented in the following section.

---

is that what you call a game?

---

game theory *Game theory* is the study of decision making under conflict situations in which more than one decision maker is involved, with each trying to maximize his utility or minimize his disutility. The name "game theory" is borrowed from similar situations which arise in common parlor games, such as chess, bridge, tic-tac-toe, or matching pennies. The model of game theory can be applied in many areas, such as military strategy, politics, and economics.

number of players Games can be classified by the number of players as *two-person games, three-person games,* or *n-person games.* In games with three or more players (*n*-person games), coalitions can be formed where the members of the coalition act for their common interest against an opponent or opponents.

number of strategies Another classification distinguishes *finite games,* with a finite number of strategies for the players, from *infinite games,* in which an infinite number of strategies are present.

zero-sum games A third classification is related to the outcomes. *Zero-sum games* are games in which the combined outcome for the players is zero. For example, in a two-person game, the gain of one player is always nonzero-sum games identical to the loss of the other. *Nonzero-sum games* are games in which this is no longer true, and the gain of one player in a two-person game, for example, is not equal to the loss of the other. This is often the case because the players associate different utilities with the same outcomes. This is demonstrated in the example that follows.

The game theory model. Figure 65 represents a two-person game. Three strategies S_1, S_2, and S_3 are open to the decision maker on the left, who is labeled player 1, and four strategies, OP_1, OP_2, OP_3, and OP_4, are open to his opponent, who is called player 2. The twelve numbers in the matrix, called the *payoff matrix*, indicate the amount paid by player 2 to player 1. The amounts may represent rewards or the utilities of the rewards corresponding to any of the possible outcomes.

    payoff matrix

As an example let us suppose that Player 1 represents Shell Oil gas stations and player 2 represents Standard Oil stations. Both Shell and Standard are considering construction of new gas stations. Shell is considering three regions in town and Standard is considering the same three regions as well as a fourth. The regions are identified by the rows and the columns of the matrix. Each plans to build only one station. The numbers in the payoff matrix represent the percent of business Standard will lose to Shell. Negative numbers indicate a gain to Standard from Shell. For example, outcome (S_1, OP_1) indicates a 12% gain by Shell from Standard when they each build a new gas station in region 1, while outcome (S_3, OP_4) indicates a 7% gain by Standard from Shell when a shell station is built in region 3 and a Standard station in region 4.

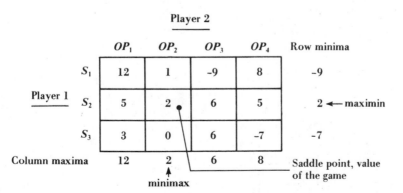

		OP_1	OP_2	OP_3	OP_4	Row minima
	S_1	12	1	-9	8	-9
Player 1	S_2	5	2	6	5	2 ← maximin
	S_3	3	0	6	-7	-7
Column maxima		12	2	6	8	Saddle point, value of the game

Player 2

minimax

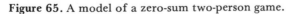

Figure 65. A model of a zero-sum two-person game.

zero-sum
game

nonzero-sum
game

maximin
criterion

When the 12% gain in business represents an increase in utility to Shell which is identical to the decrease in utility to Standard who is losing this 12% of the business, we have a *zero-sum* game. If each player assigns different utilities to the outcomes, and the gain in utility to one is not matched by a corresponding loss in utility by the other, we have a *nonzero-sum* game. Most real life situations are nonzero-sum games, because seldom do people agree on their assignment of utilities to outcomes. In fact, no transactions would be possible if this were not so. For example, when I buy a car for $6000 from a dealer, between the two of us we still have the $6000 and the car. I gained a car and the dealer gave it up, and I gave up $6000 that the dealer gained. If only concrete objects are considered, then gains equal losses and we have a zero-sum situation. But each of us believes he has a higher *utility* after the exchange or else we would not proceed with the exchange. So we both realized an increase in utility, and my increase in utility *is not* matched by an equal loss to the dealer. We both have a gain and thus the situation is a *nonzero-sum* game.

Game theory assumes that the players subscribe to the maximin criterion as the decision rule for selecting their strategies. No claim is made that this is the best criterion; rather, this is the assumed criterion in game theory. Although this criterion was viewed earlier as the cautious pessimist attitude in decisions under uncertainty, it is important to point out that the situation is somewhat different in the game theory model. In decision under uncertainty, we may have no reason to believe that nature is out to get us, and that a state will be selected on the basis of how much it could hurt the decision maker. On the other hand, in the game theory model the opponent is viewed as a malevolent creature that is out to get you, and this justifies the cautious maximin criterion.

Consistent with the maximin criterion, player 1 records the row minima and selects the maximum of these, as shown in the column on the right of the payoff matrix in Figure 65. He therefore selects strategy S_2. The opponent wishes to minimize the amount he must pay player 1. He also wishes to achieve this by the cautious maximin approach in which his choice of a strategy minimizes the worst that can happen to him. Since he is at the paying end of the game, he records the column maxima in a row below the payoff matrix in Figure 65, and of these he selects the minimum. This is the minimax. On that basis, player 2 selects strategy OP_2.

Although player 2 finds the minimum of the column maxima (minimax), it is essentially a "maximin" criterion; that is, he is choosing the best of the worst outcomes. The reason he computes the minimax is because he is at the paying end.

Both players use the pessimist's cautious *maximin* approach in the sense that they cannot be worse off. Should one of them abandon this approach and select a different strategy than that dictated by the maximin criterion, then the other player may be even better off. For example, should player 2 select a strategy different from OP_2, while player 1 sticks to S_2 then player 1 may obtain 5 or 6 instead of 2. Similarly, if player 1 abandons the maximin criterion and player 2 sticks to his, player 2 may pay only 1 or 0 instead of 2.

The value 2 in Figure 65 is called the *value of the game,* or the *solution of the game.* The intersection point of strategies S_2 and OP_2, which leads to the outcome 2 (solution of the game), is called a *saddle point.* At the saddle point the outcome is the maximum of its column and the minimum of its row. A game with a saddle point is also referred to as a game with an *equilibrium solution.* value of game saddle point

The game of Figure 65 is not a *fair game* because player 2 loses 2 units and player 1 wins 2 units each time the game is played. This is not to be confused with the concept of *zero-sum game,* which it still is because what player 1 wins and what player 2 loses add up to zero. The game of Figure 65 can be changed into a *fair game* by subtracting 2 units from each entry in the payoff matrix. The value of the game would then be zero. A fair game is a game whose value is zero. fair game

Games with no saddle point—mixed strategies. The game of Figure 66 has no saddle point because the maximum of the row minima does not coincide with the minimum of the column maxima. There is no outcome entry in the payoff matrix which is both its row minimum and its column maximum. By the maximin criterion, the players choose strategies S_2 and OP_1. However, player 2 can reason that since player 1 plays by the maximin criterion, he himself would be better off playing OP_2. In that case he will pay only 4 instead of 5. Similarly, player 1, knowing what player 2 might think, will play S_1 to obtain 6 instead of 4. This circular reasoning may go on forever, and therefore, there seems to be no equilibrium.

A famous theorem of game theory proves that for every two-person zero-sum game, equilibrium can be reached if mixed strategies are allowed. Consider a game with n strategies for player 1.

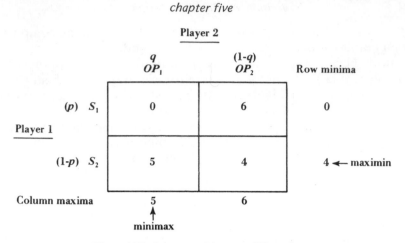

Figure 66. A game with no saddle point.

pure strategy A *pure strategy* is a scheme in which *only one* of these strategies is played with probability of 1, and all the other strategies are not mixed played at all. A *mixed strategy* consists of a scheme in which a strategy probability different from 1 is associated with the use of each available strategy. For example, a mixed strategy for player 1 could be a scheme in which two coins are tossed, and if two heads appear he plays S_1; otherwise, he plays S_2. The probability of playing S_1 would be 1/4 and the probability of playing S_2 would be 3/4. The mixed strategy in this case is denoted in the form (1/4, S_1; 3/4, S_2). Similarly, player 2 could use a mixed strategy (1/8, OP_1; 7/8, OP_2) by playing OP_1 when 3 heads appear in the toss of three coins; and playing OP_2 otherwise.

Generating the mixed strategy. In Figure 66 player 1 will try to increase the maximin of 4, and player 2 will try to decrease the minimax of 5. It is reasonable that equilibrium, if it can be reached at all, will be somewhere between these two values. A mixed strategy will reach the equilibrium state. Such a strategy is generated on the basis of the following reasoning:

Player 1. Since I have no idea what player 2 will do, but I know criterion for that he is out to get me, let me be cautious and assure myself mixed that no matter which strategy he plays, I shall realize the same strategy *expected value of utility*. This, then, is the criterion that I shall use for a game with no saddle point. Suppose I play S_1 with probability p, and S_2 with probability $1 - p$. Then if player 2 plays OP_1, my expected value of utility, EV(player 1), will be

$$\text{EV(player 1)} = p0 + (1 - p)5$$

and if he plays OP_2,

$$\text{EV(player 1)} = p6 + (1 - p)4$$

Since I want these two results to be equal, I shall equate them and solve for the value of p that achieves this equality.

$$p0 + (1 - p)5 = p6 + (1 - p)4$$
$$p = 1/7$$

Hence, my mixed strategy is

$$(1/7, S_1; 6/7, S_2)$$

and my expected value of utility is

$$\text{EV(player 1)} = (1/7)0 + (6/7)5 = 30/7$$

Player 2. Since player 1 is my opponent, I had better be cautious and assure myself the same expected value of loss in utility, irrespective of which strategy he plays. This will be my criterion. So suppose I play OP_1 with probability q, and OP_2 with probability $1 - q$. Then if player 1 plays S_1, I have an expected loss, EV(player 2):

$$\text{EV(player 2)} = q0 + (1 - q)6$$

and if he plays S_2,

$$\text{EV(player 2)} = q5 + (1 - q)4$$

Since I want these results to be the same, I shall equate them and solve for the value of q that achieves this equality.

$$q0 + (1 - q)6 = q5 + (1 - q)4$$
$$q = 2/7$$

Hence my mixed strategy is

$$(2/7, OP_1; 5/7, OP_2)$$

and

$$EV(\text{player } 2) = (2/7)0 + (5/7)6 = 30/7$$

Thus the value of the game at equilibrium is $30/7$.

Keeping your next move a secret.   It is important that your opponent does not know beforehand what strategy you are going to play on any given trial. Otherwise he could take advantage of this knowledge. In order to keep your strategy a secret, it is safest not to reveal it even to yourself! Since each player in Figure 66 can calculate the mixed strategy of the other, that cannot be kept a secret. However, you can delay till the last moment the use of a chance device that generates your strategies with the probabilities that you have calculated. A chance device for the game of Figure 66 might be the random drawing of one of seven blocks, each with a different number. For player 1, if block 1 is drawn he uses S_1, otherwise he uses S_2. For player 2, block 1 or block 2 will lead to OP_1, otherwise OP_2 is chosen. Before a player uses the chance device, the choice of an action is as much a secret to him as it is to the opponent. What you do not know you cannot give away.

Dominance.   There are situations in which one strategy is equal or superior to another on an entry-by-entry basis in the payoff
dominated strategies matrix. In such cases, we say that the superior strategy is *dominant* and we eliminate the *dominated* strategy from the matrix. For example, when we compare S_1 and S_3 in the payoff matrix of Figure 67, we note that $3 > 2$ and $6 > 5$ so that S_3 is *dominant* over S_1. Hence we can eliminate S_1 from the matrix, and reduce the game to the matrix shown in Figure 68. Similarly, in the matrix shown in Figure 69 OP_2 dominates OP_3, OP_4, OP_5, and OP_7, because player 2 is at the paying end. He therefore reduces the game to the matrix shown in Figure 70.

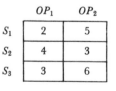

	OP_1	OP_2
S_1	2	5
S_2	4	3
S_3	3	6

Figure 67.

180

	OP_1	OP_2
S_2	4	3
S_3	3	6

Figure 68.

	OP_1	OP_2	OP_3	OP_4	OP_5	OP_6	OP_7
S_1	−6	−1	1	4	7	4	3
S_2	7	−2	6	3	−2	−5	7

Figure 69.

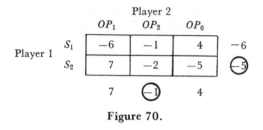

Figure 70.

if I only thought before I acted...

Alex made his way quietly into the classroom through the open door in the back. He was 15 minutes late but he had alerted his uncle in advance that he might not make the class on time. The Professor had just completed a brief review and discussion of the key concepts which were listed on the blackboard:

- zero-sum game
- nonzero-sum game
- maximin criterion
- pure strategy
- mixed strategy

181

There again was the magical number—seven plus or minus two—only five lines were on the blackboard.

Professor Gordian placed a transparency on the overhead projector, and Figure 71 appeared on the screen.

"It's story time," started Professor Gordian. One could sense the focus of attention—eyes sparkling, heads raised, necks stretched out—as soon as the word "story" was mentioned. Professor Gordian claimed, as always, "This, of course, is a true story, as are all my stories—even the ones I make up.

"Some years ago I befriended a lawyer in his early sixties. This lawyer was a most personable, pleasant, and wise person—and he loved to tell true stories from his rich experience. One day Adeline, the wife of a client, approached him and sought his advice, not in his capacity as a lawyer, but rather as a friend whose wisdom she appreciated and whose discretion and confidence she trusted.

"Adeline and her friend, Susan, had decided to go to a fashionable restaurant for lunch. On the morning of the designated day, Adeline remembered that she had no money in her purse, so she took a $50 bill from a drawer and put it in the top of her purse. Then she took her youngest son to school while her husband was getting ready to leave for work.

"The two women met at the restaurant and had a lively conversation. They had been friends for more than a decade. When they got to the dessert Adeline got up to go to the restroom and she asked Susan to keep an eye on her purse. After Adeline returned to the table, Susan got up and asked Adeline to keep an eye on her purse. As Susan disappeared on her way to the restroom, the waiter placed the bill on the table and walked away. As Adeline opened her purse to take out her $50 bill for payment, she turned white

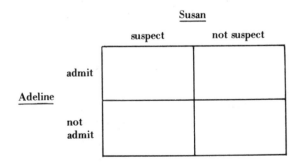

Figure 71. The tale of Susan and Adeline.

from shock. The $50 bill was gone. She was so sure that it had to be in the top of her purse, just as she had placed it in the morning, that she could not believe her eyes. She became angry, reached for Susan's purse, and without hesitation opened it. On top was a $50 bill. It looked to her just like the $50 bill she had placed in her purse that morning. She took the bill, closed the purse, signaled the waiter, and paid for lunch. When Susan returned, Adeline told her she had paid already and had to be going to pick up her youngest son from school.

"Shortly after Adeline returned from school with her son, the telephone rang. Her husband was calling to tell her that five minutes after she had left the house in the morning he had discovered that he had no money in his wallet so he had opened her purse and taken out a $50 bill that was on top. He was out of the office visiting a client but he had wanted to reach her so she would not worry when she discovered that the money was missing from her purse.

"Adeline was at a loss. What was she to do? Should she or shouldn't she tell Susan what she had done? Did Susan suspect her of stealing her money or didn't she suspect?

"Well, class, that's the story. An abstract representation is shown in this model (Figure 71). Take a few minutes and discuss Adeline's dilemma. How should she rank the four outcomes? Use 4 for the most preferred outcome and 1 for the least preferred."

The class turned into the usual beehive of activity. Everyone was talking and arguing at once. Alex watched the group next to him. Nancy, a member of the group, suggested the following ranking of outcomes for Adeline: $4 > 3 > 2 > 1$. This is shown in Figure 72.

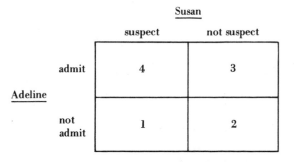

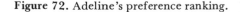

Adeline's Preference Ranking
4>3>2>1

Figure 72. Adeline's preference ranking.

Professor Gordian called for the attention of the class. "When you have completed the ranking of the outcomes from Adeline's point of view, rank them by taking Susan's position. Please continue your discussions."

Professor Gordian walked out to the hallway and Alex joined him. "How exciting," commented Alex. "There is so much human feeling, drama, and serious thinking in this story. Is it really true?"

"Does it matter, Alex?"

"I guess not, but if Adeline only had a will to doubt and considered the consequences before she had proceeded to open Susan's purse!"

"Yes," responded Professor Gordian, "but she didn't take our problem solving class. If she had she would still be working with the model when Susan returned, and I would have lost a great true story."

When Alex returned to his seat he saw Nancy write the following ranking of outcomes for Susan: $4 > 3 > 2 > 1$. This matrix is shown in Figure 73.

Nancy raised her hand and spoke. "If I were Adeline I would use the *admit* strategy regardless of what Susan would do."

conditional
strategy
A hand went up and Bill spoke. "I would act differently. If I were Adeline I would elect a *conditional strategy* in response to Susan's action. If Susan were to voice suspicion I would admit; otherwise not." Bill rank ordered the outcomes in the payoff matrix differently from Nancy.

All at once a number of students spoke up, suggesting different strategies for Adeline and Susan. There was a great deal of talk about friendship, trust, guilt, short term versus long term implica-

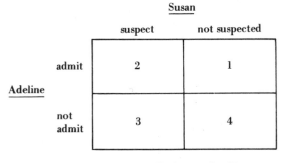

Susan's Preference Ranking
4 > 3 > 2 > 1

Figure 73. Susan's preference ranking.

tions of the choice of actions, and the nature of the future relationship between Adeline and Susan. Finally, the bell rang just as a student asked what the Professor's lawyer friend told Adeline.

"This I will make known next semester in the course Problem Solving Two," said Professor Gordian laughingly, and he dismissed the class.

Alex walked with Professor Gordian to his office. He was curious about the idea of *conditional strategies*. He also wanted to ask about a *one-sided prisoner's dilemma* model that he had encountered in his readings, along with *preference deterioration*. When they entered the office Professor Gordian looked at his mail. On top was a book that had just arrived entitled *Decisions Decisions* by Bell and Coplans. He opened it and looked at the table of contents and at the index. Then he let some pages spring from his thumb which was pressing against the edge of the book and stopped at the heading "The Doctor's Dilemma."

"Look at this, Alex, this is interesting."

Two pages of the book were devoted to an example of a surgeon–patient conflict. The surgeon had a choice of running some tests not in agreement with his better professional judgment in order to guard against a loss in case of a malpractice suit, or taking the risk of not running the tests. The patient could elect to sue or not to sue the doctor. The ranking of the outcomes is given by the payoff matrix of Figure 74.

The higher the preference of the outcome the higher the rank, with 4 being best and 1 worst. The first and second number in each box represent patient and doctor rankings, respectively.

"What do you think of this, Alex?"

"What a coincidence! This is a prisoner's dilemma," reacted

Doctor

		not test	test
Patient	not sue	(3,3)	(1,4)
	sue	(4,1)	(2,2)

Figure 74. Patient versus doctor.

Alex. "If each looks out for himself, the doctor will run question-
able and costly tests and the patient will proceed with costly malpractice suits. Mutual trust of *not test* and *not sue* would give
them each a more preferred outcome. Sad story!"

Professor Gordian closed the book. "Well, Alex, you had some
questions."

"Yes," responded Alex. "When I read the material in your book
on game theory and some articles on conflict resolution, I came
across a number of concepts that I want to discuss with you.
These are:

- A one-sided prisoner's dilemma
- Preference deterioration
- When should a player announce his position first
- Conditional strategies
- Games that include threats and promises."

"Alex, these are the subjects I plan to discuss in class next time,
but we can start now if you wish."

"No, in that case I'll wait for the class because I had intended to
attend it anyway. How about a walk through the sculpture garden
on our way to the cafeteria for a cup of coffee?"

"Good idea, Alex," said the Professor as he got up. The two left
the office.

---

why can't we all be alike?

Professor Gordian was writing on the blackboard in kingsize letters
when the bell signaled the beginning of class. He turned and greeted
the class in his customary "good morning class," to which the class
responded laughingly with a stretched out "g-o-o-d m-o-r-n-i-n-g
t-e-a-c-h-e-r."

Professor Gordian pointed to the blackboard and said: "Today we shall discuss the following topics:

- One-sided prisoner's dilemma models
- More on group and individual values
- Preference deteriorations

Here is the first model." He turned on the overhead projector and Figure 75 appeared on the screen.

"The first number on the left in each outcome represents the utility for player A, and the number on the right is the utility for player B. Therefore the outcome $(4,3)$ in row 1, column 1 is best for A, the outcome $(2,4)$ in row 1, column 2 is best for B, and the outcome $(1,1)$ in row 2, column 1 is the worst for both A and B.

"Now, class, take a minute to study these outcomes and establish whether either player has a *dominant, sure-thing strategy*."

After a brief discussion, a student spoke. "Player B has a *dominant sure-thing strategy* in column 2. He is better off choosing column 2 regardless of what player A does. If A selects row 1, then B gets 4 instead of 3 units by choosing column 2 instead of column 1. If A selects row 2, B gets 2 instead of 1 by adhering to his dominant sure-thing strategy." dominant sure-thing strategy

"What about player A? Does he have a dominant sure-thing strategy?" asked the Professor.

"No," responded a number of students. One student continued, "A's choice is *conditioned* on what B will do. If A knew that B will use column 2 then he would use row 2. But if B were to use column 1 instead, then he would use row 1."

"Good" said Professor Gordian. Then he summarized, "B has a

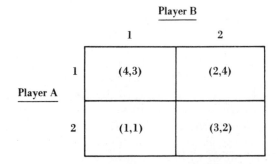

Player B

	1	2
1	(4,3)	(2,4)
2	(1,1)	(3,2)

Player A

Figure 75. A one-sided prisoner's dilemma.

187

dominant sure-thing strategy, as in the prisoner's dilemma model, one-sided while *A* does not have one. Such a game is known as a *one-sided prisoner's dilemma,* because one side only has a dominant sure-thing strategy."

Professor Gordian called on Abe and Beth to come to the blackboard, and as they were making their way to the front of the class he said: "Abe, you'll take the position of player *A,* and Beth, you'll take player *B*'s position. Please start a dialogue on what your choice of strategy will be. At the end of the class I will ask you to write down your *actual* choice. You start, Beth."

Beth: I am going to choose column 2 because this is my dominant sure-thing strategy and I think I ought to use it.

Abe: In that case I'll select row 2 and the outcome will be (3,2). If I were in your place I would abandon the sure-thing strategy and choose column 1. If you did that we would have (4,3) as the outcome.

Beth: But why should you end up with the maximum possible utility of 4 and not I, when I have a sure-thing strategy in column 2? If you think that I will choose column 1, you will have an incentive for choosing row 1. If I disappoint you and stick to my sure-thing strategy of column 2, then too bad for you. I'll get 4 units and you will get only 2 units.

Abe: Beth, you are not helping me to develop trust in you. I'll stick to row 2 and you will get 2 at best. But let me try to appeal to your group spirit. Outcome (4,3) has the maximum utility as measured by us jointly. If you look at the next best joint outcome it's (2,4), in which you gain a unit and I lose 2, so as a group we would lose 1. So. . .

Beth: Abe, you are confusing me. Now I am afraid that we will end up with (1,1) when we finally make our selections at the end of the hour.

Abe: But that is the outcome we definitely wish to avoid. It represents the lowest utility to us individually and collectively.

Beth: I agree. But the only way we can guarantee this is by me selecting column 2 and you choosing row 1. That is my point. After all, I have a dominant strategy in column 2.

Abe: But if this is your attitude, Beth, then I shall choose row 2.

Beth: Now where is *your* group spirit? Abe, have a heart. Row 1, column 2 gives us the outcome (2,4), while row 2, column 2 gives us (3,2). It seems you would rather gain one unit of utility while I lose two units. Collectively we would have five instead of six units.

Abe: You are now using the argument that I used when I tried to convince you to play column 1 instead of column 2. I asked you to cooperate and said I would choose row 1 if you chose column 1. But you indicated that you would rather have the outcome (2,4) than (4,3), thus gaining two units while I lose one. Collectively we lose one unit by going from a total of seven to six.

Beth: I somehow feel that the outcome (2,4), at the intersection of row 1 and column 2, is what we ought to settle for. I see no reason why I should take column 1 because then you will surely get four units and I will get only three. I don't have to take that risk.

Abe: But if that's how you feel about the situation, then I'll take the risk and choose row 2. In fact, there is no point in continuing the discussion. I hereby announce my intention to select row 2 and you do as you please.

Beth: You're making me angry. You know, I might retaliate by changing my mind and choosing column 1. That will really hurt you, because you will then get only one unit instead of three, a loss of two units for you. As for me, in response to your announced intention to select row 2, I will get one unit instead of two by choosing column 1 instead of column 2, which is only a loss of one unit.

"Very good" interrupted Professor Gordian. "I suggest we stop here." Abe and Beth returned to their seats. Professor Gordian presented the payoff matrix of Figure 76 on the screen and said: "The model you see now has no dominant strategy for either player S or player C. Please pair up and take the positions of S and C. Discuss your attitudes and then each of you write your choice of strategy on a piece of paper."

Player C

		C_1	C_2
	S_1	(4,1)	(2,2)
Player S			
	S_2	(1,4)	(3,3)

Figure 76.

The class erupted in the usual loud discussions all at once. After ten minutes Professor Gordian turned to the class. He called on Shigeru, an engineering student from Japan, and Cathy, an economics major from California. "Shigeru, you take the position of player S, and you, Cathy, take the position of player C," suggested Professor Gordian. Shigeru started the dialogue.

Shigeru: The outcome (S_2, C_2) has the maximum total gain *for us*, Cathy. I believe that I would be expected to choose S_2.

Cathy: I believe outcome (S_2, C_1) is best for me, and if I thought you would choose S_2, I would choose C_1.

Shigeru: But then I would choose S_1. In fact, with S_1 I can get four or two, whereas with S_2 I can only get one or three. Shigeru walked over to the left end of the blackboard and wrote:

	$C1$	$C2$
S_1:	4	2
S_2:	1	3

In S_1 the 4 is three units more than the 1 in S_2, and the 2 in S_1 is only one unit less than the 3 in S_2. I might as well choose S_1 but I would rather that you would cooperate so that we could agree on (S_2, C_2).

Cathy: We can achieve (S_2, C_2) only through mutual trust.

Shigeru: Well, I will take S_2, and if you fail me this time by choosing C_1 I will have learned something about your attitude. You then would have gained one unit, and I will have lost two, but you will lose my trust in future conflict situations.

Cathy: You are putting me on the spot, Shigeru. I think that business is business, and each is to look out for himself. You are bringing into consideration concern for *mutual trust* and for *us* while I am focusing on *my own* gains. Let me think about it.

Professor Gordian was speaking now. "What we have just witnessed is of great importance. Shigeru started by focusing on the group and what is best for the two collectively. Cathy reacted from her own frame of reference. It is even possible that two cultures were represented by the two attitudes. You may recall how Shigeru once told us that in Japan, when one is asked what he thinks about an issue, he is most likely to tell you what would be expected of him. The group affiliation and the group objectives are most important. You may also recall that Cathy was surprised to hear that, and felt that one has the obligation to express his or her own opinion and not the expected opinion. This is why I called on them to take sides in this game."

"Who is right then?" asked a student.

"There is no absolute right or wrong strategy in this case," responded Professor Gordian. "The answer depends on the culture, the values of the players, on the short as well as long term implications of the choice, and if the players are concerned about the future relationship. There are times when it is reasonable to take the risk of short term losses in order to gain the trust of an opponent for future encounters.

"Thank you, Shigeru and Cathy. Now before turning to our last example for today, let's ask Abe and Beth to write down their choices of strategies for their game, and Shigeru and Cathy to write down their choices for the last game."

All heads turned to the four students. Each wrote the chosen strategy and handed it to Professor Gordian.

"I'll announce the results next time," said Professor Gordian mischievously. Sounds of disappointment were heard from every corner.

"Come on, Professor Gordian, tell us," cried out Nancy.

"O.K., here are the choices," responded Professor Gordian, who had not really intended to keep the results a secret.

"Abe's choice: Row 1
Beth's choice: Column 2
The outcome: (2,4)"

The class booed the result.

Abe looked at Beth and jokingly said: "You traitor!"

Professor Gordian continued,

"Shigeru's choice: S_2
Cathy's choice: C_2
The outcome: (3,3)"

The class cheered.

Professor Gordian placed a new transparency on the projector. Figure 77 appeared on the screen. "Now, class, take a few minutes to discuss this situation."

After ten minutes had passed Professor Gordian spoke. "Let us begin with some questions. First, how will player A rank the four outcomes?"

John responded:

"A_2, B_1 : $(\underline{1},1)$ Worst
A_1, B_2 : $(\underline{2},2)$ better
A_1, B_1 : $(\underline{3},4)$ better yet
A_2, B_2 : $(\underline{4},3)$ best"

191

Player B

	B_1	B_2
A_1	(3,4)	(2,2)
A_2	(1,1)	(4,3)

Player A is labeled on the left.

Figure 77.

"And player *B*?" asked Professor Gordian.

Cathy answered, "*B* will agree with *A* on the worst and next to worst, but will reverse the order of best and next to best. (A_1, B_1) is best for *B*, while (A_2, B_2) is best for *A*."

"What should *A*'s strategy be?" asked Professor Gordian.

"If I were *A*," said Beth, "I would announce quickly, before *B* had a chance to convey his position, that I will choose A_2 and would then cut all communications with *B*. This would force *B* to choose B_2, unless he was mad enough to choose B_1 under these circumstances."

"But *B* could do the same by jumping the gun on *A* and announce a strong uncompromising position choosing B_1 first, thus forcing *A* to choose A_1," reacted John.

"That's true," responded Beth. "That's why, in this game, you should act fast and in a seemingly irrational manner. The crazier you appear, the more uncompromising, the better."

"But you may have two equally stubborn players," suggested someone, "and then they will end up with what both consider as the worst outcome."

preference deterioration "These observations are quite to the point," said Professor Gordian. "When a player becomes angry and feels the other should yield, he may reach a state in which his own preferences begin to deteriorate and he develops the attitude of 'over my dead body will you get the advantage.' If player *A* takes this attitude, he may convince himself that he prefers (A_2, B_1), the worst for both, as compared to what is best for *B*, which is (A_1, B_1). It is as if the values 3 and 1 in column 1 have changed places (reducing Figure 77 to 78). This would make A_2 appear as a dominant sure-thing strategy to *A*.

"If *B* remains rational, he may yield by choosing B_2, which will

192

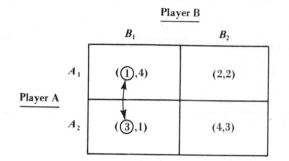

Figure 78. Deterioration of preferences for Player *A*.

lead to (A_2, B_2), his second best outcome. But should *B*'s behavior match that of *A*, he may prefer (A_2, B_1), which is the worst for both, to (A_2, B_2) which is *A*'s best. It would be as if (in Figure 78) the 1 and 3 of row A_2 in columns B_1 and B_2, respectively, had changed places (reducing Figure 78 to 79). B_1 would then become a *dominant, sure-thing strategy* for *B*.

"This situation (Figure 79) will lead *A* to choose A_2, and *B* to choose B_1, and they will settle for what really is their worst outcome. Think about these results before our next meeting." He then wrote the assignment for the next class meeting and dismissed the class.

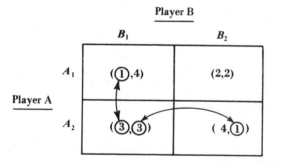

Figure 79. Deterioration of preferences for *A* and *B*.

should I really study the model before I commit the crime?

Later, in Professor Gordian's office, Alex continued the discussion of conflict situations. Professor Gordian drew Alex the model of Figure 80 in response to Alex's questions about *threats, promises,* and *conditional strategies.*

conditional strategy

"You see, Alex, in this model (Figure 80) we have a *conditional*

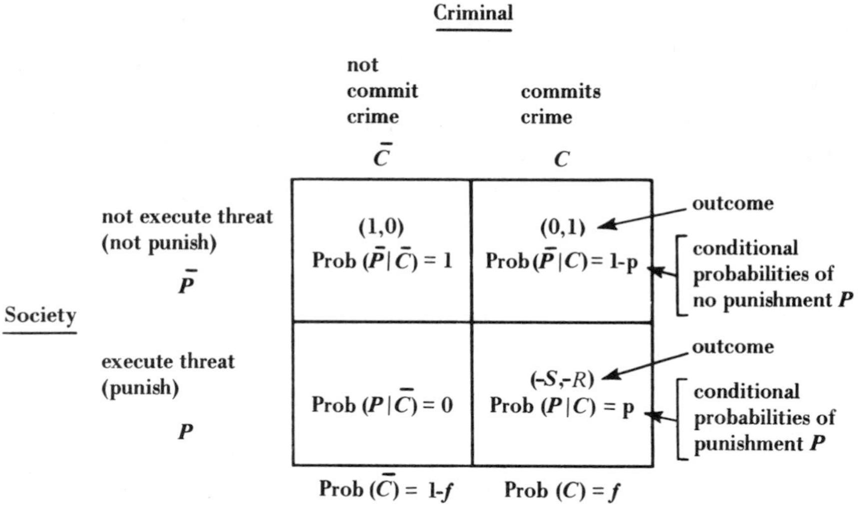

Criminal

	not commit crime $\bar{C}$	commits crime C
not execute threat (not punish) $\bar{P}$	(1,0) Prob $(\bar{P}|\bar{C}) = 1$	(0,1) Prob $(\bar{P}|C) = 1\text{-}p$
execute threat (punish) P	Prob $(P|\bar{C}) = 0$	(-S,-R) Prob $(P|C) = p$

Society

Prob $(\bar{C}) = 1\text{-}f$ Prob $(C) = f$

outcome — conditional probabilities of no punishment P

outcome — conditional probabilities of punishment P

Figure 80. A model for a conditional strategy.

response to his choice of C, which is a criminal act against society. This would cause the criminal a loss of R, while society would sustain a loss S in applying the threat. This would be outcome (P,C). If the criminal behaves and chooses $\bar{C}$, society promises not to execute the threat and chooses $\bar{P}$. Then society has one unit and the criminal has zero, yielding the outcome $(1,0)$. If the criminal commits the crime by choosing C and society does not execute its threat of punishment, then the criminal takes the unit away from society, yielding the outcome $(0,1)$ at $\bar{P},C$.

"So society threatens to use P if the criminal uses C, and the criminal may choose $\bar{C}$ or C in full knowledge of the threat.

"Now the threat can be either a success or a failure. Do you see which outcomes correspond to these states, Alex?"

"Yes," answered Alex. "Success means that the criminal will not commit a crime; i.e., he chooses $\bar{C}$, and society will not execute the threat. So $(\bar{P}, \bar{C})$ corresponds to success. Failure means that the outcome is (P,C) or $(\bar{P},C)$.

"We can get more sophisticated with this model," said Professor Gordian. "Suppose that when crimes are committed society executes its threat of punishment P with a probability Prob $(P|C) = p$. Then the criminal can get away with his crime with no punishment with a probability $(1 - p)$. In this case, if the criminal has taken our problem solving course he will reason as follows:

If he does not commit the crime and chooses $\bar{C}$, he has an outcome of 0.

If he commits the crime by choosing C, then he has an outcome of 1 with probability $1 - p$, and an outcome $-R$ with probability p

The total expected value of committing the crime is $(1 - p)$ $(1) + (p) (-R)$

"For a threat to be effective so as to deter the criminal from committing the crime, the expected value of C should be smaller than the expected value of $\bar{C}$, that is

$$(1 - p) (1) + (p) (-R) < 0$$
$$1 - p - (p) (R) < 0$$
$$1 - (p) (1 + R) < 0$$

or

$$1 < (p) (1 + R)$$

and

$$p > \frac{1}{1 + R}$$

So here is a relationship between the probability of society executing the threat and the severity of punishment R to the criminal. This relationship explains what is necessary for society's threat to be effective against crime on the basis of our simple model. It should help society to balance the punishment R and the probability p of executing the punishment. This also should help a criminal who has taken our problem solving class decide what to do.

"Suppose R is 1. Then from the above relationship $p > 1/2$, that is, the threat must be executed no less than half the time. But if the punishment R is very severe, say 1000, then the threat should be executed with a lower bound of $1/1001$. So we see that if the punishment is not severe then it should be applied more frequently than when it is severe. Or if the threat is executed very often, then the punishment may be less severe than when threat is not executed very often to achieve a certain level of deterrence to crime."

"Is there also an upper bound on p?" asked Alex.

"Yes," responded the Professor, "this will depend on the probability of failure of the threat and on the loss, S, to society in executing the threat. Would you like me to generate this bound? It is more complicated than what we have done so far."

"Go ahead," responded Alex, "this is interesting. You see, in the back of my mind I am trying to relate all this to the story of the man who was holding the hostage, and the police who were trying to work out a deal for his safe release, with threats and promises flying all over the place. Perhaps this model can help me deal with this problem."

"OK, Alex," said the Professor. "Suppose the threat fails with probability f. The criminal therefore uses C, i.e., commits the crime, with probability f, $\text{Prob}(C) = f$. The threat is a success with probability $1 - f$, i.e., $\text{Prob}(\overline{C}) = 1 - f$.

"Society reasons as follows: when the threat is a success and the criminal chooses $\overline{C}$, which he does with probability $1 - f$, $[\text{Prob}(\overline{C}) = 1 - f]$ then society does not execute the threat and must choose $\overline{P}$ with a probability of 1. $[\text{Prob}(\overline{P}|\overline{C}) = 1]$ thus obtaining the outcome $(1,0)$ at $(\overline{P},\overline{C})$. So the expected value for society when the threat is a success is

$$(1 - f)\,(1)$$

When the threat is a failure and the criminal uses C, which he does with probability $\text{Prob}(C) = f$, then society will either apply the threat with probability p, $[\text{Prob}(P|C) = p]$ and have an outcome of $-S$ units, or will not apply the threat with probability $1 - p$, $[\text{Prob}(\bar{P}|C) = 1 - p]$ and have an outcome of 0. The expected value for society is therefore

$$(f)(p)(-S) + (f)(1 - p)(0)$$

or

$$-fpS$$

The overall expected value from the threat is therefore

$$(1 - f)(1) - (fpS)$$

or

$$1 - f - fpS$$

"With *no threat,* namely, a policy of no punishment regardless of whether the crime is committed or not, society would expect zero, since the outcome will be $(0, 1)$, i.e., $(\bar{P}, C)$, because it is always to the criminal's advantage when society's choice is $\bar{P}$.

"Therefore, for the threat to be worthwhile, the expected value to society from the policy of threat should be larger than from a policy of no threat to punish, that is

$$1 - f - fpS > 0$$

or

$$1 - f > pfS$$

or

$$\frac{1 - f}{fS} > p$$

"So here is the upper bound on p. Combining the two bounds we have

$$\frac{1 - f}{fS} > p > \frac{1}{1 + R}$$

Therefore, how often the threat is to be executed, i.e., the probability $p_* =$ Prob$(P|C)$, depends on the probability of failure of the threat, $f =$ Prob(C) the punishment to the criminal represented by R, and the cost to society in executing the threat represented by S."

"This is a little complicated, but very interesting as a tool for thinking about complex social problems," said Alex. "I have to get a better appreciation for the implications of S, R, f, and p in real life situations. I'll try to come up with some examples and discuss them with you."

---

some people are takers,
some are givers...

"Here is one more example that you may want to study, Alex," said Professor Gordian. "It uses our two-person game model to study the individual and his relationship to the group. Let us take, for example, ten people who live in a small community. Suppose the community as a whole can pay out ten units, one per person, and realize a gross return of 30 units of benefit for a net gain of 20 units to the community. We assume for simplicity that there is a gross return of three units for each unit paid, and that the overall gross gain is shared equally by all ten members of the community regardless of whether a member participated in the investment or not. For example, if one person contributed and nine did not, the gross return to the community would be three units. Dividing three by ten, then 0.3 units are received by each member. However, the one who made the only payment for the good of the community paid out one unit and received only 0.3 units, so he realizes a net loss of 0.7 units.

"On the other hand, if nine members each contribute one unit and one member does not, the overall gross return is $9 \times 3 = 27$ units. These 27 units are distributed to all ten members, and we have 2.7 units per person. For each of the nine contributors the net payoff is 2.7 – 1.0 = 1.7, since they each paid out one unit. The one member of the community who did not pay his share receives a net payoff of 2.7 units. Situations like this may arise when people are asked to contribute their share on a voluntary basis for a project which is enjoyed by the entire community."

Alex opened his notebook, and taking his pen started to sketch a model for the situation that Professor Gordian had described.

"I believe I can identify the numbers you have generated as elements of a payoff matrix in this figure." He pointed to Figure 81. "We consider one individual in conflict with a group of nine. If all cooperate and pay their share, each gets a two unit net payoff. If all defect, each gets no net gain. If the individual pays and all nine others do not, he is in for a loss of 0.7 units, and each of the other nine receives a net gain of 0.3 units. If the individual defects and does not pay, while all others do, he receives a net gain of 2.7 units while each of the others gets only 1.7 units."

"Very good, Alex," said Professor Gordian, who then asked, "What can we conclude from this model? Will the individual cooperate?" Alex paused for a minute, then answered, "The individual has a dominant sure-thing strategy in *not pay,* i.e., *defect,* with 2.7 and 0 respectively representing higher payoffs than the corresponding 2 and –0.7 units when he cooperates. So he will defect." Alex looked puzzled as he completed his answer, and then continued, "But there is a paradox here. Each member of the group of nine seems to have a dominant sure-thing strategy in *cooperate* because 2.0 and 1.7 are better than 0.3 and 0 respectively."

"Wait, Alex," responded the Professor, "we treated the nine

Group of 9

		cooperate (pay)	defect (not pay)
Individual	cooperate (pay)	(2,2)	(-0.7,0.3)
	defect (not pay)	(2.7,1.7)	(0,0)

Figure 81. Net payoffs for the individual and for each member in the group of nine.

199

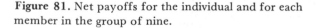

members of the community as a single entity. If each of them places himself in the position of the *individual* in our model, playing against the remaining nine he will reach the same decision as our individual, namely, defect and you will be better off. You can control your own action, but you have no complete control over the actions of others. Of course, in smaller groups, you may exercise better control through peer pressure than in larger groups."

"But wouldn't our individual feel guilty letting others pay while he does not pay and is enjoying an equal measure of the reaped benefits?" asked Alex.

"That is a good point, Alex," said Professor Gordian, "but what is the other extreme possibility?"

"Well," answered Alex, "he may be the only one paying, and then feel like a fool knowing that he sustained a net loss while everyone else was enjoying his 'good deed'."

Professor Gordian got up and said, "Alex, let me leave you with some food for thought. You may stay here and work on the problem because I must go to a meeting. Here are two questions: *First:* Is it possible that the benefit will be so large for a single payment that the individual may elect to pay regardless of what the others in the community will do? *Second:* Suppose we leave the return on investment as it is, namely three units gross return for each unit invested. Also suppose we divide the community into two groups. Each group has the complete cooperation of its own members, but the two groups are in conflict with each other. How will the payoff matrix change as we progress with the division of the community of ten into the following sets of two groups?

	Row Group	*Column Group*
Division one	1 member	9 members
Division two	2 members	8 members
Division three	3 members	7 members
Division four	4 members	6 members
Division five	5 members	5 members

Professor Gordian left the office and Alex started working on the two problems. For the first problem he thought he would consider a return high enough to offset the loss of 0.7 units to the individual, and make everyone's return larger than 0. He tried five units of gross return but it did not work. He inspected Figure 81 again. "I have it!" he thought to himself, "If the individual pays and all others do not, he is out one unit. Everyone will receive the same gross benefit, except that the investing individual will have to deduct his investment while the others have no investment to deduct. So the gross gain for each of the ten members must be more than one unit if the investing individual is to have a net gain." He tried a gross return of 11 units for each unit invested, and generated the payoff matrix of Figure 82.

Group of 9

	cooperate (pay)	defect (not pay)
Individual cooperate (pay)	(10,10)	(0.1,1.1)
defect (not pay)	(9.9,8.9)	(0,0)

Figure 82. Net payoffs for a gross return of 11 on each unit invested.

His calculations appeared on the page as follows (individual action, group action):

(Pay, Pay):   all 10 pay, $11 \times 10 = 110$ gross return

$110/10 = 11$ gross gain for each

-1 payment by each

$11 - 1 = 10$ net gain/person

(Not Pay, Pay):   9 pay, $9 \times 11 = 99$ gross return

$99/10 = 9.9$ gross gain to each

$9.9 - 1 = 8.9$ net gain to each of 9 (who paid)

$9.9 =$ Net gain to individual who did not pay

(Pay, Not Pay):   1 pays, $1 \times 11 = 11$ gross return

$11/10 = 1.1$ gross gain to each

$1.1 - 1 = 0.1$ net gain to one who paid

$$1.1 = \text{Net gain to each of others (who did not pay)}$$

(Not Pay, Not Pay):   0,0

"Interesting," Alex thought to himself, "the individual has a dominant sure-thing strategy in cooperating regardless of what the other nine do, and this will be true for gross returns larger than ten units for each unit invested. When the gross return is smaller than ten, *defect* is dominant for the individual, and at a gross return equal to ten he will be indifferent between cooperate and defect."

Alex then started to generate the results for the second question considering a gross return of 3 units for each unit invested. He noted on his page:

For *Row Group* of 2 and *Column Group* of 8

(Pay, Pay)   All cooperate = (2,2)

                    30 gross gain = 3/person

                    payment   = 1/person

                    net gain   = 2/person

                    All defect   = (0,0)

(Pay, Not Pay)   Row Group of 2 pays 2

                    gross return   = 2 × 3 = 6

                    gross return   = 6/10 = 0.6/person

                    net return in
                    Row Group   = 0.6 – 1 = –0.4/person

                    net return in
                    Column Group   = 0.6/person

(Not Pay, Pay)   Column Group of 8 pays 8

                    gross return 8 × 3   = 24

                    gross return 24/10   = 2.4/person

                    net return in Row Group   = 2.4/person

                    net return in Column Group 2.4 – 1 = 1.4/person

Alex's results are summarized in Figure 83.

Alex prepared payoff matrices (Figures 84, 85, and 86) for 3 more cases and filled in the values (2,2), (0,0) for the outcomes in the upper left box and the lower right box. He performed the following calculations as he filled in other values:

3 pay	3 × 3 = 9	9/10 = 0.9	0.9 – 1 = –0.1
7 pay	7 × 3 = 21	21/10 = 2.1	2.1 – 1 = 1.1
4 pay	4 × 3 = 12	12/10 = 1.2	1.2 – 1 = 0.2
6 pay	6 × 3 = 18	18/10 = 1.8	1.8 – 1 = 0.8
5 pay	5 × 3 = 15	15/10 = 1.5	1.5 – 1 = 0.5

Alex reviewed Figures 83 to 86 and made the following note:

For a group of 2	*defect* is dominant
For a group of 3	*defect* is dominant, but less than for a group of 2
For a group of 4	*cooperate* is dominant
For a group of 5	*cooperate* is dominant, but more than for a group of 4

"Enough for one day," Alex said to himself. He wrote a note to Professor Gordian thanking him for the instructive and illuminating lesson of the day, attached his worked out solutions to the Professor's two questions and then left the office with a feeling of great satisfaction in how much he had learned in one day.

Column Group - 8 people

	cooperate (pay)	defect (not pay)
Row Group 2 people — cooperate (pay)	(2,2)	(-0.4,0.6)
defect (not pay)	(2.4,1.4)	(0,0)

Figure 83. Group of two versus group of eight.

Column Group - 7 people

	cooperate (pay)	defect (not pay)
cooperate (pay)	(2,2)	(-0.1,0.9)
defect (not pay)	(2.1, 1.1)	(0,0)

Row Group
3 people

Figure 84. Group of three versus group of seven.

Column Group - 6 people

	cooperate (pay)	defect (not pay)
cooperate (pay)	(2,2)	(0.2,1.2)
defect (not pay)	(1.8,0.8)	(0,0)

Row Group
4 people

Figure 85. Group of four versus group of six.

Column Group - 5 people

	cooperate (pay)	defect (not pay)
cooperate (pay)	(2,2)	(0.5,1.5)
defect (not pay)	(1.5,0.5)	(0,0)

Row Group
5 people

Figure 86. Group of five versus group of five.

Later that evening he summarized his ·new found knowledge in his intellectual diary:

SUMMARY

1/ Game theory deals with decision under conflict, i.e., where the outcome of a decision depends on the action of a malevolent opponent. Game theory can be used to analyze many different types of decision under conflict, including not only games, but military strategy, business strategy, and economic and political theory.

2/ Decision under conflict situations can be modeled with a payoff matrix. One player's actions are listed as a row variable, and the other player's actions are listed as a column variable. The outcome of each combination of actions is listed as the cell entry.

3/ In a zero-sum game, the amount won by one player is the same as the amount lost by the other. In a nonzero-sum game, these amounts do not have to be the same. For a zero-sum game, the single entry in each cell represents the amount the first player (row) is paid by the second player (column). In a nonzero-sum game, there are two entries in each cell. The first entry represents the payoff to the first player (row) and the second entry represents the payoff to the second player (column).

4/ The usual game theory strategy is the maximin criterion. Each player looks for the worst possible outcome that can occur for each course of action available to him, and then he picks the course of action that has the best of these worst possible outcomes. This is a reasonable approach since it is assumed that there is a malevolent opponent who will take the utmost advantage of whatever course of action is employed.

5/ A dominated strategy is one in which each outcome is worse than in some other strategy no matter what action is taken by the opponent. A dominated strategy should therefore never be played, because there is at least one other strategy that is always better.

6/ A saddle point exists in a zero-sum game when the maximin strategy of one player yields the same payoff as the maximin strategy of the other. This payoff is the value of the game.

7/ A fair game exists when the payoff at the saddle point is zero; that is, neither player is winning or losing anything.

8/ Some games do not have a saddle point. In such games a solution can be reached by adopting a mixed strategy instead of a pure strategy. A pure strategy is one in which a player consistently plays only one of his possible strategies or courses of action. In a mixed strategy a player plays some probabilistic combination or two or more strategies. The criterion used in a mixed strategy is that the mixed strategy should lead to the same expected value of outcome regardless of what the opponent does. In a mixed strategy it is important that the opponent not know exactly which course of action will occur on the next trial, so that he cannot anticipate it and take advantage.

9/ A prisoner's dilemma is a type of nonzero-sum game in which each player has a dominant, sure-thing strategy, that is, a strategy in which the outcome is better than any other strategy regardless of what the opponent does. In a prisoner's dilemma, the adoption of the dominant, sure-thing strategies by both of the players will lead to an outcome that is not of mutual best benefit.

10/ A one-sided prisoner's dilemma occurs when only one player has a dominant, sure-thing strategy, while the other player has a conditional strategy. A conditional strategy is one in which the optimal course of action varies depending on what the opponent does. In a one-sided prisoner's dilemma the outcome resulting from one player playing his dominant, sure-thing strategy is not of mutual best benefit.

11/ Arriving at the mutually optimal outcome in a prisoner's dilemma depends on adopting a collective rationality arising from mutual trust, as opposed to an individual rationality that would lead each player to adopt his dominant, sure-thing strategy.

12/ Preference deterioration can sometimes be observed in nonzero-sum games. One player may become frustrated because the opponent fails to cooperate and arrive at the mutually optimal outcome. The other player may convince himself that he would rather receive an even worse outcome for himself just to ensure that his opponent does not benefit.

13/ The TiGeR can be used to analyze prisoner's dilemma type problems. There is a *temptation* (T) for each player to defect, given that the opponent will cooperate. There is some *gain* (G) from mutual trust, as opposed to no gain or even loss from mutual defection. Also, there is a *risk* (R) associated with trusting your opponent, since he may defect.

PROBLEMS

1/ Look at the reduced payoff matrix in Figure 68, page 181.
   a/ Is there a saddle point? Why?
   b/ Determine the optimal strategies for each player.
   c/ What is the value of the game?

2/ Consider a game in which each of the two players, A and B, writes on a piece of paper 'H' or 'T,' and then they compare their choices. If both wrote H, player A receives one dollar from player B. If both wrote T, A receives three dollars from B. If their choices do not match, A pays B two dollars.
   a/ Complete the following payoff matrix:

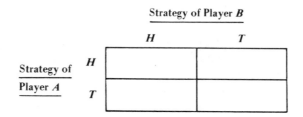

Figure 87. Payoff matrix for Problem 2.

   b/ Find the mixed strategy for player A.
   c/ Find the value of the game.

3/ For the following game, determine if there are dominated strategies and cross them out. Then from the resulting payoff matrix, determine the following:
   a/ The optimal strategy for A.
   b/ The value of the game.
   c/ Can A obtain a higher payoff than the value determined in (b)? Explain.

		Player B 1	Player B 2	Player B 3
Player A	1	1	7	7
Player A	2	8	5	2
Player A	3	10	6	3

Figure 88. Payoff matrix for Problem 4.

4/ Look at the payoff matrices given on pages 183 and 184. Analyze this situation.

5/ Look at the payoff matrix on page 185. Use the TiGeR to analyze this situation.

6/ Consider the situation described on page 173. Imagine the situation in detail, or use a similar real life situation that you are aware of, and use the game theory model to analyze it.

PROJECT

Consider some real life conflict that can be modeled with the game theory tools discussed in this chapter. This could be a personal conflict of yours or a more general social conflict. Some examples might be a conflict you have with a friend or your family, conflict in a business situation, or a conflict between countries. Set up a payoff matrix with alternative courses of action for both parties, assign utilities, and discuss the problem in terms of the concepts introduced in this chapter.

annotated bibliography

Adams, James L. *Conceptual Blockbusting: A Guide to Better Ideas.* Freeman: San Francisco, 1974.
> A very readable little book that gives a wealth of examples illustrating blocks to problem solving and how to overcome them. It discusses creativity and creativity enhancing techniques. Paperback.

Bell, Robert, and Coplans, John. *Decisions Decisions: Game Theory and You.* Norton: New York, 1976.
> Another short, easily read book that discusses the everyday applications of game theory. It gives many realistic examples to illustrate the broad uses of game theory. Hardcover.

Carnap, Rudolph. *Philosophical Foundations of Physics: An Introduction to the Philosophy of Science.* Basic Books: New York, 1966.
> More than just a book about physics. Carnap gives a lucid exposition of the philosophy of science by utilizing physics as an example. The book discusses models of physical science and theory formation and testing. Hardcover.

Davis, Gary A. *Psychology of Problem Solving: Theory and Practice.* Basic Books: New York, 1973.
> Davis discusses some theory and many applications of problem solving techniques, with an excellent survey of group problem solving and creativity enhancing techniques. Hardcover.

Howard, Nigel. *Paradoxes of Rationality: Theory of Metagames and Political Behavior.* The MIT Press: Cambridge, 1971.
> An advanced book on games with conditional strategies called metagames. The book identifies three categories of breakdown in rationality encountered in decisions under conflict. Hardcover.

Kaufmann, Arnold. *The Science of Decision Making.* McGraw-Hill: New York, 1968.
> Although a fairly technical, theoretically oriented treatment, this book gives examples of a wide variety of decision making models and techniques. Paperback.

Keeney, Ralph, and Raiffa, Howard. *Decisions with Multiple Objectives: Preferences and Value Tradeoffs.* Wiley: New York, 1976.
> An advanced exposition on the multiattribute decision problem, like Alex's problem of what car to choose. Keeney and Raiffa explore the intricacies and subtleties of the multiattribute decision problem and give a detailed derivation and discussion of more sophisticated models. Hardcover.

Koberg, Don, and Bagnall, Jim. *The Universal Traveler, A Soft-Systems Guidebook to: Creativity, Problem Solving, and the Process of Design.* William Kaufman, Inc.; Los Altos, Calif., 1974.
> An inventive book which covers the cognitive aspects of the problem solving process. It gives numerous suggestions for improving problem solving and creativity. It has a heavy "pop" format, but it is fun to read. Paperback.

Laszlo, Ervin. *The System View of the World: The Natural Philosophy of the New Developments in the Sciences.* George Braziller: New York, 1972.
> A short book describing systematic scientific thinking and modeling. It gives specific applications to several different areas of inquiry. Hardcover.

Mager, Robert F. *Goal Analysis.* Fearon Publishers: Belmont, Calif., 1972.
> This delightful little book focuses on the need to eliminate fuzzies and to be precise by setting performance measures in all types of problem solving. Paperback.

Mosteller, Frederick, Rourke, Robert, and Thomas, George. *Probability with Statistical Applications.* Addison-Wesley: Reading, Massachusetts, 1961.
> An excellent introduction to probability for those who want to pursue the topic in more depth. It is very well organized and gives many useful examples and applications. No calculus is required. Paperback.

Lindsay, Peter, and Norman, Donald. *Human Information Processing.* Academic Press: New York, 1972.
> Could well serve as an introductory psychology text, with a heavy emphasis on the psychological aspects of problem solving. It also treats decision making and language and communication. Hardcover.

Polya, G. *How to Solve It.* Doubleday: New York, 1957.
> Polya gives a systematic method for enhancing your ability to solve mathematical problems. There are numerous examples. Paperback.

Raiffa, Howard. *Decision Analysis.* Addison-Wesley: Reading, Massachusetts, 1968.
> This book treats in considerable detail the problems of making decisions under risk and uncertainty, as well as other topics. It gives a detailed treatment of decision trees. Paperback.

Rubinstein, Moshe F. *Patterns of Problem Solving.* Prentice-Hall: Englewood Cliffs, New Jersey, 1975.
> A comprehensive treatment of problem solving and decision making, with a treatment of many other useful topics, including modeling, probability, language, computers, and values. Hardcover.

Schelling, Thomas, C. *The Strategy of Conflict,* Harvard University Press: Cambridge, Mass., 1960.
> An excellent book that presents a sophisticated, but mostly nonmathematical, treatment on choice of strategies in conflict situations. Hardcover.

Wickelgren, Wayne A. *How to Solve Problems: Elements of a Theory of Problems and Problem Solving.* Freeman: San Francisco, 1974.
> A theoretical treatment of psychological processes in problem solving, with many examples utilizing specific problem solving guides. Paperback.

answers to selected problems

Chapter 1

5/ A common constraint is to try to divide the land into only rectangular plots. Try triangular plots.

6/ A common constraint is to use only straight lines. Try curved lines.

7/ The first clue regarding the product of the ages leads to the following combinations of integers:

    1,1,36
    1,2,18
    1,3,12
    1,4,9
    1,6,6
    2,2,9
    2,3,6
    3,3,4

The clue regarding the sum of the ages must refer to the following possible sums:

$$1 + 1 + 36 = 38$$
$$1 + 2 + 18 = 21$$

$$1 + 3 + 12 = 16$$
$$1 + 4 + 9 = 14$$
$$1 + 6 + 6 = 13$$
$$2 + 2 + 9 = 13$$
$$2 + 3 + 6 = 11$$
$$3 + 3 + 4 = 10$$

Note that there are two identical sums of 13. That is why the last clue is needed. The statement: "The *oldest* has red hair" establishes that 2,2,9 is the answer.

8/ To obtain the shortest distance unfold the room into a flat representation by leaving the wall with the fly connected to the ceiling only and the opposite wall with the jelly connected to the floor only. A straight line from the fly to the jelly drawn on the flat representation gives the shortest distance of 40 feet.

9/ Start with a special case of 1 disc, then 2, then 3, and identify a pattern. The answer for 8 discs is 255 steps.

10/ 6 days

Chapter 2

8/ *C*'s hat is black. You can use the method of contradiction to show that *C*'s hat cannot be white.

10/ There are 20 distinct paths.

11/ a/ Valid
b/ Invalid
c/ Invalid
d/ Invalid
e/ Invalid
f/ Invalid

12/ The set of girls with brown eyes lies within the set of girls without blonde hair. Since 70% of all girls have brown eyes, then between 70% and 100% of the girls do not have blonde hair.

Chapter 3

3/ a/ 13/52
b/ 4/52

  c/ 1/52
  d/ 16/52
  e/ 4/52, 4/52
  f/ 0
  g/ 8/52

4/ a/ 4/45
  b/ 4/36

5/ 2 to 43

6/ 5/6

7/ a/ Independent, not mutually exclusive
  b/ Independent, not mutually exclusive
  c/ Dependent, not mutually exclusive
  d/ Dependent, mutually exclusive
  e/ Independent, not mutually exclusive

8/ a/ 4/9
  b/ 1/3
  c/ 3/4
  d/ 1/4
  e/ 19/36
  f/ 17/36

9/ $4 (0.3) (0.7)^3$

10/ $\$1/6 \approx 17\cancel{c}$

11/ Fair price is the expected value of $\$1/3 \approx 33\cancel{c}$

12/ a/ 45$\cancel{c}$
  b/ lose 15$\cancel{c}$

13/ $\$7/9 \approx 78\cancel{c}$

14/ a/ 0.86
  b/ 0.047
  c/ 0.0025

15/ a/ 0.63
  b/ 0.37

16/ a/

		Vote		
		Democrat	Republican	
Party affiliation	Democrat	480	120	600
	Republican	40	360	400
		520	480	

216

b/ 120/480
c/ 120/600
d/ 480/600, 360/400
e/ Democrats

17/ a/

	Cancer	No Cancer	
+	4.75	99.5	104.25
−	0.25	895.5	895.75
	5	995	

Test (label at left, between + and − rows)

d/ 4.75/104.25 = 0.0456
e/ 0.312
f/ 0.80

18/ a/ 1/2
b/ less than 1/2
c/ $\dfrac{(1/2)^{11}}{1/2 + (1/2)^{11}} = 0.001$
d/ $\dfrac{0.999\,(1/2)^{10}}{0.999\,(1/2)^{10} + 0.001} = 0.49$
e/ 1. Without the will to doubt new evidence is not taken into account.

19/ a/ Divide uncertainty in half
b/ 3 questions
c/ 4 3/8

20/ a/ Divide uncertainty in half
b/ 2 1/4
c/ 2 13/32 when questions start with most probable route
6 1/16 when questions start with least probably route

Chapter 4

1/ a/ Using probability of 1/4 for each state of nature, plant tomatoes
b/ Plant nothing
c/ Plant asparagus
d/ Plant peas when 50% optimist and 50% pessimist
e/ Plant tomatoes

2/ a/ Using probability of 1/3 for each state of nature, skim notes
   b/ Skim notes
   c/ Watch TV
   d/ Skim notes when 50% optimist and 50% pessimist
   e/ Skim notes

3/ a/ Treat
   b/ Wait

4/ Auto 2

Chapter 5

1/ a/ No saddle point because maximin of player 1 is not equal to minimax of player 2.
   b/ For player 1 $p(S_2) = 3/4$ and $p(S_3) = 1/4$.
   For player 2 $p(OP_1) = 3/4$ and $p(OP_2) = 1/4$.
   c/ 3 3/4

2/ a/

	Player B H	T
H	1	-2
T	-2	3

Player A

   b/ $p(H) = 5/8, p(T) = 3/8$
   c/ -$1/8 = -12 1/2¢

3/ a/ A should use row 1 and row 3 with probabilities 7/13 and 6/13, respectively.
   b/ 5 2/13
   c/ Yes, if he knows in advance what *B* will do.

4/ Dominant strategies are *sue* and *test*. The gain from co-operation is 1 unit (3-2). The temptation to defect is 1 unit (4-3), and the risk of cooperation is 1 unit (2-1).

index